Real Leadership

Through the Heart

Frank Noble

This Edition Published in 2019

IBSN 9781076379832

Independently Published

Copyright © Frank Noble 2019

The stories in this book do not use true names, in order to preserve anonymity.

For Debbie and Jake

and the dogs who have shared our lives,
Barney, Scooby and Bodie

Thank you for your love and support

Dedicated to the everyday leaders who lead
through engaging the hearts of real people
... intended or unintended

CONTENTS

The author 1

The origin of the book 4

Preface - How to get the most from this book 11

1 **Real Leadership** The heart of the matter 14

2 **Reflection** A reflection 18
Personal growth 24
Preparation 28
Impressions 31

3 **Tone** A reflection on tone 32
Tone 41
Manner 44
Conversations 46
Expectations 48

4 **Context** A reflection on context 50
Context 55
Time 56
Location 58
Information 59
Stakeholders 62

5 **Leading** A reflection on leading 64
Your essence 73
You leading 76
Decision making 80
Adapting 84
Communicating 87

6	**People**	A reflection on people	91
		People	98
		Individuals	99
		Teams	102
		Energy	111
		Change	113
7	**Success**	A reflection on success	116
		Success	127
		Winning	130
		Challengers + opponents	131
		Mistakes and failure	134
8	**Military Leadership**	A reflection on leadership	137
		Command	139
		Leading	141
		Headquarters	144
		The boss	146
		Orders	147
		Comradeship	149
		Discipline	150
	Postface - You		152
	Real Leadership Forum - Facebook group		154

THE AUTHOR

Real Leadership - Through the Heart is drawn from a lifetime of experience during which I was called upon to be a leader, soldier, commander, manager, director, coach, engineer, agony aunt, mentor, counsellor, trainer and magistrate.

Through a career spanning 31 years, I led individuals and teams of all shapes, sizes, creeds and cultures. I led small tactical teams and large corporate-scale organisations. I commanded the Northern Ireland engineer regiment and the British Army's Air Support engineer brigade.

Over every continent (except Antarctica), I led international teams in Afghanistan, Australia, Belize, Bosnia, Canada, Cyprus, Germany, Gibraltar, Kenya, Kuwait, Nepal, Northern Ireland, North Sea, Norway, Oman, Sierra Leone and the South Atlantic.

For 9 years, I volunteered as Chairman of Army Rugby League. I led the annual inter-services rugby league campaign against the Navy and Royal Air Force. I drew tremendous insight from working alongside managers, coaches and players at club, national and international level.

I embraced the many training and personal development opportunities that were available in the British Army. The highlights were a Master of Science degree in the Design of

Information Systems, an Advanced Management course at the Alliance Manchester Business School and the Defence Strategic Leadership Programme at the Cranfield School of Management.

I graduated from the Royal Military Academy Sandhurst in 1985 and went directly to the Commando Course at the Royal Marine training centre in Lympstone, Devon. I joined the Royal Engineers and qualified as a Military Engineer through the Royal School of Military Engineering, Chatham. Over the next 31 years, I rose to the rank of Brigadier (known as Brigadier-General in most armies around the world). During that time, I led multi-disciplined professional teams delivering a diverse range of capabilities, skills and services, including:

➢ Air support (airfields for military planes and helicopters).

➢ Bomb disposal (as it sounds).

➢ Commando forces (support to the Royal Marines).

➢ Diving (military underwater search and engineering).

➢ High risk search (finding bombs).

➢ Infrastructure and estates (military training facilities).

➢ Maritime counter-terrorism (support to the Special Forces).

➢ Military equipment procurement and support.

➢ Military engineering (civil engineering in uniform).

➢ Public order (riot control).

➢ Range safety (military firing ranges).

- ➢ Recruiting (soldiers and civilians).
- ➢ Training and education (engineering apprentices).

I loved every moment of the 31 years.

I miss the people.

THE ORIGIN OF THE BOOK

The genesis of this book lay in the sands of Saudi Arabia.

It was a warm windy evening in the eastern desert of Saudi Arabia, an hour from the Persian Gulf port of Al Jubail and a 6 hour drive south from the border with Kuwait. The date was Sunday 4th November 1990. I was deployed on an operation that would become known as the First Gulf War.

As I sat in my Landrover, sheltered from the wind and sand by a camouflage net sewn onto a green parachute, I was filled with a feeling of dread and foreboding. I had come to believe that an absence of leadership in the command team above us would lead to the death or injury of soldiers in our unit. I set about writing a daily journal, believing that one day it would be read at an inquest.

I had passed out of the Royal Military Academy Sandhurst in 1985, completed a 9 month engineering course at the Royal School of Military Engineering in Chatham and had been posted to an armoured engineer regiment in Nienburg, Germany. I had spent 2 wonderful years driving armoured engineer tanks around the streets and fields of Germany. We were kept busy preparing for the day when the Warsaw Pact forces would drive westwards. Our task was to block their advance. We practised laying 'pretend' minefields and preparing 'pretend' demolitions of the big road/rail bridges over the German rivers and canals. It was an exhilarating time. As I finished that posting, the Berlin Wall started to come down and the Cold War thawed.

Life got even better when I was posted as the Troop Commander of 2 Commando Troop in the bomb disposal and search regiment. It was a true privilege to lead a group of dedicated, professional, motivated and highly capable commando-trained engineers. Life was busy. We spent 3 months in Norway every year on arctic warfare training, supporting 3 Commando Brigade. When we were back in the UK, we were at a constant state of readiness to provide 'high risk search' support to the UK Special Forces maritime counter-terrorism operation. As part of that operation, we were responsible for finding potential bombs and booby traps on UK ships and oil/gas platforms. We even managed a 3 month deployment to Gibraltar, where we cleared World War 2 munitions from land that had been reclaimed from the sea by the Gibraltar government (the sand had been reclaimed from a munitions dumping ground on the sea bed, by mistake). As a troop, we became highly proficient at deploying around the world, preparing ourselves, training ourselves and delivering operational capabilities.

We now found ourselves in the desert sands of Saudi Arabia, commanded by a squadron that had very limited experience of operational deployments. We were deployed alongside a Parachute Troop and a Chemical Troop.

From the moment we arrived in Saudi Arabia, the squadron command team had little to offer in terms of direction, guidance and co-ordination. Initially that felt good, as we enjoyed the freedom to organise our own troop routines. However, as the storm clouds of war gathered, the absence of leadership from above became disconcerting and alarming. The troops were left to develop their own operating procedures around how to conduct patrols, night security routines, anti-ambush drills, tactical vehicle movement and bomb disposal incident procedures.

We had arrived by RAF aircraft ahead of the allied ships. Once the ships arrived, it quickly became clear that the squadron had too much equipment to fit into our Landrovers and trailers. It was left for the troops to decide what equipment to take with us.

I was starting to get quite concerned. We were ready to deploy, vehicles were loaded and yet the squadron command team was not letting us have the tools of our trade: ammunition, explosives, morphine. We were poised to deploy into the desert, but did not have the means to defend ourselves or to dispose of munitions. Did the command team understand what they were doing? Did they trust us? Despite our repeated requests, nothing was forthcoming and no explanation was offered.

We heard that a higher level regimental command group meeting was being held, where instructions would be given for the squadron to move into the desert alongside other units. I was too junior to attend. As I was settling into my sleeping bag for the night, I received a surprise summons to the command tent to write the orders for the squadron to move into the desert the next day. I thought that I was being asked to work alongside the boss, to help him think through the orders. In the event, he did not appear (gone to bed). It took me a couple of hours to find out what orders had come down from the regiment earlier, before I could set about writing the orders for the squadron. A few hours later, after sunrise, it felt a little odd to be sat amongst the troop commanders, receiving orders for the move from the boss (orders that I had written). I did not tell anyone.

Things did not improve once we were established in the desert. On Sunday 11th November 1990, the nearby engineer regiment decided to hold a Remembrance Service in the desert and invited the squadron to join them. The service was to be held half a mile away across soft sand. The squadron command team decided to form us up in neat lines, as if we were on a parade square, and march us over the sand to the service. It was impossible to march in time. The squadron command team persevered in their attempt to march us as one group, in time. The shouting got louder and louder. The scene resembled something out of Monty Python, as an operational bomb disposal squadron attempted, and failed, to march in time over soft sand. The assembled rows of regimental officers and soldiers looked on bemused as we staggered into view, red faced. We all wished that the ground would open and swallow us up.

By this stage, we were intent on getting away from the command team for the sake of our sanity and safety. The Chemical Troop found their way back from the desert to Al Jubail port where they offered their bomb disposal support to the logistics base. The Parachute Troop found themselves at the desert artillery firing ranges, where they disposed of any munitions that had not exploded.

As a troop, we busied ourselves with training, firing our weapons and helping out at the artillery range. The mail was getting through. We seemed to be getting more information from the letters and newspapers arriving from our families than we were getting from the squadron command team.

As the D Day drew near, I moved the troop to a desert quarry, where we could establish a dug-in defensive position, with overhead protection. I informed the squadron command team where we had moved. They did not seem to mind.

It had been raining for days and was getting quite cold. One evening as I was wrapped up warm and snug in my sleeping bag, the troop signaller burst in and tipped me off my camp bed, screaming 'Scud, Scud, Scud'. The war had begun, with the Iraqi forces firing Scud missiles towards the port and our desert positions. The chemical alarms sounded and we all dived into our chemical suits.

Once the initial fuss had subsided, we received instructions from the squadron command team. I was to drive 2 hours back through the desert to the port, through the Scud alerts and chemical attack sirens, to pick up our ammunition, explosives and morphine. It turned out that the squadron command team had been storing it all in a metal shipping container at the port!

My lifelong interest in leadership had begun ...

In the event, it was a relief that the conflict did not unfold the way we had feared. The Iraqi air force was comprehensively suppressed by the allied air forces and we did not have to clear unexploded Iraqi air-dropped bombs. However, we did have to clear quite a few unexploded bombs and bomblets that had been dropped by allied forces on to Iraqi Army positions. Thankfully, we did not face the widespread use of chemical or biological weapons against us.

The troop was called out of the desert midway through the conflict to support the re-taking of the British Embassy in Kuwait city, via a helicopter-borne assault. Once the allied advance into Kuwait had been successful, the main task was to clear booby traps that had been left by departing Iraqi troops. The troop cleared booby traps from beaches, roads, buildings and the Kuwait City power station. We did suffer a serious casualty while clearing the beach, when an anti-personnel mine exploded in the face of one of our Sappers. Although he suffered a serious injury to his eye, he lived to fight another day.

We shook off the desert sand and returned home. I counted the same number of people back into the UK who had originally left for the war. The experience left me with a determination to study leadership, take every opportunity to improve myself and work hard to offer real leadership to real people.

PREFACE

How to get the most from this book

This book is the only book you will ever need on leadership. It captures a life time of insight and observations on real leadership that will stimulate your own unique leadership knowledge, skills and growth.

The book will help you to cultivate and invigorate your own unique leadership personality, whether you are just starting out or you are further along your leadership journey.

The book does not attempt to fill the academic space around leadership, people, group dynamics and teams. It offers a set of timeless observations and insights that will help you grow and develop whoever you are, wherever you are and whatever challenges lie ahead.

An initial reading of this book will give you an overview. Make notes as you go. Highlight. Turn the corner of the pages that interest you. Stick flags between the pages.

It is a book that will then keep on giving. Dip in and out of the sections and observations that are interesting and relevant to you, in order to stimulate your reflection, learning and growth.

Like any other craft, leadership merits regular review and practice. You will have your own interests, level of experience and personality traits. Your environment and circumstances will change over time. The book enables you to dip in and out of the observations when you need, in order to explore deeper meaning and value.

The book does not examine personal motivation and ambition. How you adjust, or even compromise, your leadership to fit your ambition is a matter for you.

There are repetitions in the book. That is deliberate. Some insights are worth repeating and reflecting on again, and again.

Stories have been used to introduce the chapters. The stories come from real life experiences and serve as reflections on the themes in the chapters. Within the stories, the characters and their actions are real, but the names have been changed in order to respect their anonymity.

This book will not suit everyone. Not everyone will get it or connect with the format. That's perfectly fine. If it stimulates your thoughts and reflection, it will have been a worthy read. Ideally, it will provide a handrail for your life-long personal leadership growth.

Above all, enjoy your journey.

CHAPTER 1

Real Leadership

*Real leadership flows through the heart of the leader,
into the hearts of others*

*Real leaders engage people through their energy,
emotional connection and personal example*

*The heart and soul of leadership is found in the inspiration of
people through the forging of emotional bonds*

The Heart of the Matter

Leadership is one of the most studied and least understood subjects in human history, due to the overwhelming bias that 'leadership is for leaders'. This is not so. Leadership is for all. It does not matter what appointment you fill, whether you work from home or in an office, whether you play sport socially or as a professional, whether you work for profit or not-for-profit, whether you feel like a leader or a follower, whether you have children or not, whether the word 'leadership' makes you uncomfortable or inspires you.

Leadership is a craft. To master a craft, you need knowledge, skills, determination and patience. Craft skills are developed through practice, review, adjustment and improvement. A craft requires practical skills to be blended with creativity and heart.

Defining leadership as a science fails to understand the central importance of heart and soul.

Defining leadership as an art fails to understand the need for study, clarity, skills and structure.

Leadership permeates all aspects of life. It is the glue that bonds people into successful teams.

Successful teams need leaders at every level.

Everyone exercises leadership at one time or another. Consciously or unconsciously, by design or by necessity, some more often than others, some more confidently and knowingly than others.

Some people find the very word 'leadership' uncomfortable, perhaps believing that it is not for them, it is not their style, not their way, or something for others.

Developing the craft of leadership is a personal endeavour and journey. Individuals develop their own style and approach depending on their personality and context. This book will help anyone striving to make their way in any walk of life: business, political, sport, education, public service, charity, training, volunteering, expeditions, military service and even parenting (leading your children).

Occupying a management position, title or role does not make you a leader.

There is an awkward relationship between leadership and management that remains unresolved. Both have their place. Ideally, leadership and management are entwined together in the persuasive genuine engagement of people alongside efficient management.

Some management activities are mistaken as leadership: directing, instructing, ordering, controlling, telling, debating, consulting or conferring. Such management activities have their place, but are not real leadership.

CHAPTER 2

Reflection

Leadership is a craft

The more time you spend honing your craft,
the more capable you will be

Practice, study and review will keep your leadership
vibrant and alive

A Reflection

The most powerful leadership experience of my life happened in the blink of an eye. It proved to be the most profound and powerful source of reflection throughout my career.

I was 22 years old and had completed 7 weeks of the British Army's officer training course at the Royal Military Academy Sandhurst. At such an early stage, I was still learning to march in time as part of a formed group. Our instructors seemed to be frustrated and amused in equal measure, as we struggled to march in time and to halt as one group. The voices of the instructors became more shrill and hoarse, as they wrestled with their new intake of 'green' officer cadets.

The first day of the course had been a severe shock to my system. I had completed a computing degree at Leeds University and enjoyed a year off with a group of friends finding temporary work to fund our social life. Life had not been very taxing. I arrived at Sandhurst with my parents and we were shown to the Indian Army Memorial Room for tea and biscuits. Even as the tea was being poured, a Colour Sergeant instructor appeared at my side. I was whisked away and driven to an accommodation block. I was enveloped in a distinct sinking feeling. It dawned on me that the contents of my four large suitcases would not fit into the slim locker that I was given. My discomfort became palpable when I was confronted by a red-faced Company Sergeant Major who wanted to know why I had turned up with 24 cans of lager!

Following a vain attempt to march to lunch, I was handed a large pile of un-ironed uniform. After being introduced to the Company Commander, we were set the task of cleaning the whole accommodation block including the toilets and showers, before ironing all of our uniform. I got to bed at 2.01 a.m. After 3 hours of sleep, the instructors burst in and announced that the Company would be inspected at 6.00 a.m. The pace had been set and we soon realised that it would be relentless.

We were immersed in a flurry of basic training. We learned to march, give first aid, read maps, clean and iron uniform, handle and fire weapons, clean toilets, stand to attention, salute and do everything in quick-time. In the local woods, we learned to live in the field, build shelters, cook on open fires and navigate at night without torches. The gymnasium was the setting for endless bouts of circuit training. The surrounding roads and hills were the landscape for endurance runs and marches, often carrying heavy rucksacks and military equipment. We did a lot of physical exercise, an awful lot.

Good work and positive effort were met with praise and encouragement. A perceived lack of effort or poor standards were met with instant physical exercises or subsequent 'show parades'. The instant physical exercises included press ups, star jumps, sits up and pull ups. A large scaffolding construction in the courtyard was known as the 'Mean Machine'. It enabled the instructors to keep a large group of cadets occupied on a variety of physical exercises. The 'Mean Machine' cast a long shadow over the Company and tested the resolve of the most determined cadets. A 'show parade' was given for a failure of standards. It consisted of reporting to the Duty Colour Sergeant late at night in spotlessly clean and ironed uniform, to be inspected. Needless to say, the instructors were looking for the smallest blemish. When you inevitably failed the inspection, you had to run off and fix the offending fault. You then returned for a further inspection. The number of re-inspections depended more on the mood of the instructor than the cleanliness of your uniform.

I understood that it all had a purpose. We all came from different backgrounds, with different life experiences and different attitudes. We were being broken down to a common basic standard, so that we could be built up again. I was pleasantly surprised in the second week, when we had our first lesson in leadership from the Company Commander - the qualities of leadership. I could already feel a sense of purpose building in the training. However, I had no idea where that first lesson would take me, who I would lead in the future, what challenges I would face, what mistakes I would make and what successes I would enjoy.

The pace was exhausting, but I was getting used to it, toughening up and even beginning to enjoy it a little. At that early stage, the practical leadership training was based around 'command tasks'. A group of 5 or 6 cadets would have a leader nominated by the instructor. The group would be presented with a pile of equipment and a practical problem to solve. We constructed aerial ropeways over imagined canyons, built rafts to move across 'shark-infested' lakes and rescued casualties on make-shift stretchers.

My turn eventually came around. We found ourselves at the assault course. I was nominated as the group leader. We had to traverse between two obstacles, without touching the ground. There were 6 of us with poles, rope, planks and a number of heavy boxes. Everyone and everything had to move across the imagined canyon without touching the ground. One mistake, someone or something touching the ground, would lead to us all going back to the start. I had done a few of these as a team member and thought that leading would be straight forward. I explained the task to the team and held a group discussion on the options. I then took the decision on how we would proceed. My confidence was high. Then reality quickly set it. People did not do what I had told them to do. People did not tie the knots well enough and planks came apart. People lost their balance and fell off. One or two people did not seem to be trying very hard. As my blood pressure and frustration rose, I found myself getting into the detail and trying to do everything myself.

Failure seemed inevitable. Then I felt it. At first it was a gentle tug. Then it became a firm pull, and finally a sharp jerk backwards. The Colour Sergeant instructor had grabbed my jacket from behind and pulled me sharply backwards. Without saying a word, he pulled me back 2 or 3 feet. I assumed that we had failed and he was ending my miserable attempt. However, he said nothing. Instead, he simply looked towards the group who were now watching and waiting for further instructions. Then it dawned on me. I had become too involved in the detail of the action and was not leading. We got the task done. I stayed a couple of feet back from the group throughout the remainder of the task. Once we had finished, I felt frustration and relief in equal measure.

I never forgot that day. The firm pull from behind. The presence of the instructor watching me from behind. I was forever in the debt of that Colour Sergeant. That moment has always served to remind me to lead with thought, look long, think broadly, be clear, plan ahead, monitor progress, adjust when necessary, keep everyone updated, allow people to get on with the tasks you have set, step in if you must but then step back as soon as you can, keep calm and have confidence in team.

That moment, the pull on my back, represented the most powerful leadership lesson I have ever learned.

Personal Growth

Start with yourself. Be mindful of the meaning and purpose in your life. Be comfortable that this will change and develop during your life. Your leadership will be richer and more resonant when you are grounded in your own self-awareness.

Study the science and art of leadership - always learning, to improve your performance. There is no limit.

Managing your impulsive emotions will be one of the biggest success factors in your life.

Know yourself through conscious reflection and development.

Development, challenge and learning are good for the soul.

The more senior you become, the more time you need to think. People are relying on you to be the thinker.

Take time to understand your passions - what fires you up, what motivates you, what sits at your core.

You cannot fool all of the people all of the time. Do not try to.

Being at the top does not mean you have reached the limit of your growth.

There are no limits to improving the margins of your own performance.

Seek out knowledge, it will help to bring understanding.

Be true to yourself. You can improve through training, coaching and education. However, if you try to be something or someone you are not, you are likely to come across as awkward, false or even untrustworthy.

The best teams have clearly expressed goals, trained hard, built a spirit and bond, nurtured individual members, learned from mistakes and celebrated their successes. You are the same. Follow that lead.

Avoid comparing your performance and achievements with others. Focus on your own performance.

Wisdom is built through knowledge, experience, reflection, trying and succeeding, trying and failing, learning to manage your emotions, patience and nurturing your curiosity.

Understand the world in which you live, both close by and in the distance.

You need your own support. Map out and nurture your own support network.

Stimulate a culture around you that approaches training, coaching and mentoring as signs of positive grounded leadership, underpinned by growth and improvement.

In seeking support, ensure you are clear on the needs. Set out the relative priorities for attention, the timeframes and the intended outcomes.

For you to benefit from support, you must be open to change, ready for the opportunity and willing to invest your time and energy.

If you are going to spend time and resources being trained, coached and educated, aim for substantial improvement.

Find your own mentors and role models - people to support you in the longer term, to understand you and to offer off-script informal advice.

If in doubt, ask. It is better to seek advice, than keep quiet and get it wrong.

Most people admire the person with the desire and confidence to ask the question that everyone else was thinking but dared not ask.

Do not be too hard on yourself. Things will not always go well. You will not always get things right. Accept it and move on. Always forward.

If you go too far or lose control, put things right by apologising and forgiving yourself.

Make a small change and repeat it each day for at least 21 days. By then you will have created a habit.

Exercise regularly, sleep well, eat well and make time to relax.

Preparation

Name a team, any team, in any profession or serious endeavour, which has achieved a challenging goal without preparation and training. There isn't one. You are the same. Do not rely on instinct and chance.

The 7 x Ps:

Prior
Planning

and   Preparation

Prevents
Pretty
Poor
Performance

Prior, planning and preparation are the most important stages. Set yourself up well and good things will follow. The reverse is true. Think long and hard about how you are set up. Be flexible. Adjust to changing circumstances but avoid change for its own sake.

Do not expect the impossible, be realistic.

The real world is complex, so simplicity is key. Break things down into simple steps and then build up. Do not allow preparation to become over complicated for the sake of it.

Focus on each step until it is being done well. Then speed up.

Always start with accuracy and quality. Then build up the energy.

Get the basics right. Practice over and over. Practice under increasing pressure, up to the level that it reflects real world pressures as closely as possible.

Success is underpinned by doing the basics well. High achievement is underpinned by consistently doing the basics really well, under pressure.

Be realistic about the time required to master something.

Going back a few steps will reinforce understanding.

Most pressure is generated from within us.

Condition yourself for moments of pressure by visualising, imagining and talking yourself through the way you see things unfolding. The more you practice, rehearse and accept the way you will feel, the more controlled you will be.

Talking yourself through an activity, providing a real time commentary, will enhance your concentration and focus.

Make objectives challenging yet achievable. Be prepared to be flexible in order to keep things on track and moving forward, while keeping people motivated and engaged.

Do not be shy with yourself. Think positively about your own performance in powerful, emotive and inspirational terms.

When faced with pressure, make positive plans. Move towards the challenge. Welcome and embrace the opportunity.

Use nerves as a positive source of focus, motivation and energy.

Confront your fears, otherwise they may hijack you at the wrong time.

The most dangerous time for mistakes is often just after you think that you have mastered something. It is easy for the focus and attention to be lost. At those moments, re-double your efforts to maintain focus, consistency and control.

Do not accept low standards through a lack of effort.

Impressions

People are not always what they first appear. There is nearly always something deeper. Sometimes there is a pleasant surprise, sometimes it is impressive or intriguing, and sometimes it is to be avoided. Do not be too quick to make judgements. Bide your time and find ways to dig below the surface.

Some people are slow starters, but can be just as powerful as people who make an instant impression. Slow burners have a place in every team.

Perceived strength often contains an unseen weakness.

Perceived weakness often contains hidden strengths.

Make quick judgements, but think through what may be unseen and have strategies for adjusting your initial view.

Your use of language will significantly influence the impression people have of you.

Foster a positive mind-set through the use of language around improvement, looking for positives, explaining what needs to be done, telling stories, avoiding absolutes and identifying options.

CHAPTER 3

Tone

Organisations and teams are a reflection of their leaders

Leaders set the tone

People adapt to the leadership tone around them

The culture follows the tone being set

A Reflection on Tone

As a soldier, the highlight of my military career in uniform was the opportunity to command 12 (Air Support) Engineer Brigade. The brigade deployed men and women to provide specialist engineer support to UK military activities in Afghanistan, Iraq, Oman, Kenya and the South Atlantic. When that role came to an end, I was posted to lead a team within Defence Equipment & Support, which procures and supports all of the UK Ministry of Defence's equipment. Some 10,000 people work on one site, just north of the City of Bristol. I was uncertain how to go about leading a large team of civil servants and contractors, with a handful of military personnel. After 2 years of intense military operations working alongside uniformed men and women, I had some reservations about this new role.

I had no idea that I would end up feeling as privileged and proud to work with this mixed civilian-military team as I had ever felt before.

I arrived at the front gate of the Defence Equipment & Support complex filled with trepidation about the challenge ahead. When I met the team on that first day, my concerns were reinforced. I did not receive a formal handover and my desk had no files. A few people were friendly but most were neutral in their welcome, while some were downright hostile. Most people seemed to work at their desk in relative silence, with their heads down. The open-plan office lacked soul with very little energy, positivity or purpose. Most of the team had left the office by 4.30 p.m. that afternoon.

As a team, we were responsible for procuring and supporting all of the equipment that was needed to build and maintain the Army's temporary camps overseas. One of those camps was Camp Bastion in Afghanistan, which grew to the same physical size as the City of Reading, with 15,000 camp beds. We supported similar camps in Afghanistan, Cyprus, Iraq, Kenya, Oman and the Falkland Islands. The temporary camps were made up of tents, flat-pack modular buildings and shipping containers modified to house showers, toilets, offices and workshops. Most significantly, we supplied the protection systems that were placed around the camps to protect the occupants from bullets, rockets, grenades and bombs.

We had a serious job to do. Lives were at stake. However, the team was in a bit of a mess. There were so many short notice operational demands from the frontline that everyone was rushing around dealing with the latest priorities of work - we called it 'fire fighting'. There was no strategic planning and very limited coordination of the day-to-day business operations. There were 12 gapped posts in a team of 60 people. Most of the team were coming into work, doing what they were told to do, keeping their heads down and going home at the allotted time.

Despite the active military operations overseas, the Defence budget was being cut in real terms each year. As a team, we were under continual pressure to do more with less.

The relationship with our industry suppliers was cold and distant, largely based on holding them to account for delivering against rigid timelines that did not always match the needs of the frontline.

After 2 weeks in the role as team leader, I took stock and wondered how to turn it all around, how to engage the team and how to ensure that we were doing our very best for the servicemen and women who were in harm's way.

I started where I had always started, with the purpose and intent. Despite some reluctance on their part, I gathered the leadership team of finance, commercial and project managers. We went back to the basics and asked ourselves questions around why we existed as a team, what was our purpose and how should we function. Rather than engage in a long drawn out process, we met on 3 occasions, concluded and then wrote an operational business plan. With everyone so busy, some managers saw the review as an un-welcome distraction and something that just seemed to be about producing a written plan. Thankfully, enough managers engaged with the review for it to be recognised as a collective effort.

Most of the elements of the plan were straight forward. We identified our mission, priorities, governance structure, people management principles and skills programme. More significantly we committed to a clear leadership approach, team development programme and team charter. I was encouraged by how much ground we covered in the review. However, at that stage I did not appreciate which element of the plan would have the most significant and lasting impact on the people in the team, their level of engagement, motivation and sense of well-being.

Rather than simply identifying our key activities and deadlines, we also identified the outputs and effects that we needed to have on the frontline overseas. The overall tone was set with a 'goal' that became the headline for all of our meetings, presentations and plans. We identified our team goal as:

"Making life better for the soldier in the field"

The effect of the tone set by this headline 'goal' was immediate, dramatic and long lasting. It connected everyone in the team with the soldiers on the frontline overseas. The job suddenly felt real and meaningful. It motivated people positively, despite the frustrations of working in a large bureaucracy with a reducing budget. It encouraged people to find solutions rather than focus on problems.

For the first time, civilian members of the team started to volunteer to accompany military members of the team overseas.

The overseas visits were designed to conduct checks and audits, as well as provide opportunities to meet end users and learn operational lessons. This became a regular feature of the team, with civilian team members undertaking training, being equipped with military protective equipment and deploying to camps in Afghanistan and Iraq. The effect of these deployments was electrifying, as the team saw their colleagues volunteering for dangerous journeys and coming back with pictures and stories of the positive effects of our collective efforts. The most powerful stories were undoubtedly around the lives being saved by the protection systems we provided for the camps and which suffered thousands of attacks. Many lives were saved and injuries prevented.

One of the most heartfelt and emotional moments came during a visit to Camp Bastion in Helmand Province, Afghanistan. I was visiting the camp to review the effectiveness of the camp protection systems, accompanied by 2 civilian members of our Bristol-based team. We were in a tent-office with the camp engineer commander when he heard that there had been an attack on a patrol and 2 critically injured soldiers were being flown back in a Chinook with the medical emergency team. A couple of minutes later we heard the distant 'thump' of the helicopter rotor blades. The sound grew louder as the helicopter closed in. It was travelling at full speed, straining every sinew to get the critically injured soldiers to the field hospital in Camp Bastion. The helicopter swooped in fast and low, flaring in a dramatic last minute movement as it touched down as quickly as possible. The

Chinook passed about 25 metres over our heads. The noise was deafening, the downdraught from the rotor blades violently shook the tent and we had to hold on to the tables to prevent them toppling. As the Chinook took off to return for the less seriously injured casualties, we were again shaken by the violent downdraught. The noise of the departing helicopter was replaced by the noise of ambulance wheels crunching on gravel as we heard the medical staff transferring the casualties from the landing pad to the field hospital. The war had suddenly become very real and very close.

On return to Bristol, the 2 civilian members of the team were transformed. They had both been positive and forward thinking individuals, highlighted by their preparedness to travel to Afghanistan. However, far from being negatively impacted by their experience, they became role models of the highest order displaying professionalism, good humour, can-do attitude and drawing great satisfaction from their work. Their positive energy and attitude was infectious amongst their team mates.

The headline 'goal' set an overall tone that was embraced and shared by the civilian and military members of the team alike. It connected the team emotionally and intellectually to the wider uniformed organisations within Defence, who had previously seen the team as lacking understanding, empathy and commitment. The tone set by the 'goal' built positive and warm relationships with other organisations where previously there had been distance, detachment and even suspicion.

Over time, individual members of the team who had been quiet and distant, came out of their shells. The open-plan office buzzed with energy and humour. People gathered around desks to solve problems and to plan. We had a new problem, as the office noise level became a distraction. We re-arranged the office to create areas where people could gather for informal meetings, without disturbing their colleagues.

The team energy and positivity began to impact our relationship with industry. Where previously it had been confrontational and transactional (we called it 'win-lose'), the project managers began to adopt relationships based on partnerships with their suppliers (which we came to call 'win-win'). While retaining a firm commercial edge, we worked together with our suppliers to deliver our goal rather than simply counting the contractual deliverables.

The team moved away from the previous 'fire-fighting' behaviours to adopt a more deliberate business-like approach in which we forecasted future demand (rather than just reacting to short notice demands), planned the supply of the future demand, adopted a portfolio management approach and embraced a formal learning review process to drive continuous improvement.

We put our leadership and team development framework into action, ran team building away days, managed a structured training programme, held weekly team reviews in the middle of the open floorplate, tracked the progress of our team maturity model and openly embraced the values within the team charter.

By the time I was posted to my next role, the team was as effective, energised, efficient and committed as any team I had worked with before. It was a privilege to work with that group of professional people.

We had brought clarity, structure and planning to the team, whilst retaining responsiveness and agility. The team had come together and bonded through the development of the individual alongside the development of the team. With those sound foundations in place, the team was able to face any challenge.

The most immediate, significant and long lasting improvements had come from the effects of adopting a simple emotional 'goal' that set a powerful tone and served to bond people around a common purpose.

Tone

Leaders set the tone, spirit and atmospherics through their thoughts, words and deeds.

Your tone will impact those above, besides and below you.

You get out what you put in.

Behaviour and energy are catching.

Over time, people increasingly reflect the energy, attitude, commitment and example of the leader.

If you are in a position of authority, people will know it. There is no need to throw your weight around. However, be firm and decisive when it is warranted.

Leadership = Do as I do.

'Do as I say' has a place, but is not real leadership.

Look the part: demeanour, posture, clothing, accessories.

Be positive. Address any negatives but focus on the positives. Build a positive and forward looking culture.

Do the right thing, rather than the easy thing or the most profitable thing.

Be a problem solver rather than a problem finder.

Value the people around you. Make sure they know the value you place in them. They will sense insincerity.

Ensure people understand the approach you are taking.

Through all of the challenges and travails, leaders must be the ones to keep things in perspective.

Be mindful of the tone you are setting and the atmospherics you are generating:

vs

Open, Informed	Closed, Secretive
Engaged, Contributing	Arms Length, Distant
Empowered	Directed
Trained, Coached	Instructed
Positive	Negative
Forgiving	Blame

Flexibility is a mind-set not a collection of job descriptions. Encourage people to ask 'why not', rather than 'why'.

The use of language is the single most powerful tool you can employ to engage people.

Think deeply about the language you use.

Language must be consistent. Be careful to avoid language that does not fit.

Body language and tone of voice usually account for the majority of what is said.

Recognise that organisations are made up of multiple teams. A mature, resilient and effective organisation is able to harness distinct identities at all levels, within an over-arching shared identity. Set a tone that enables such a framework to flourish.

The output of an organisation can exceed the sum of the parts when the different teams complement each other, foster positive competitiveness and empower individuals, within a unifying purpose.

Recognise and celebrate those things that set the team apart.

Leaders should eat last, in order to demonstrate humility, respect for others and the value they place in their team.

Manner

Walk-the-walk. Use the power of personal example.

Be relaxed but never casual. Most people are not inspired by casual.

Treat others as you would wish to be treated.

Carry your personal ambitions lightly.

Humility means having the self-confidence and self-awareness to admit you do not have all the answers and you are able to learn from others. Learn how to listen, really listen. Humility builds trust and respect.

Show respect to gain respect.

Small acts of appreciation and thanks go a very long way.

Thank you - the two most powerful words you can use.

Authentic praise, when deserved, has real impact.

Praise effort, not ability.

Praise should exceed criticism by at least 3:1.

Do not seek or expect thanks.

Learn to trust your instincts. If your *wee small voice* is saying 'I'm not sure about this one', then stop, think, check.

Be on time. Allow for potential hold ups. Arriving late for no good reason will not fill your host or colleagues with admiration or thanks. If you are going to be late, inform your host as early as possible. It is just manners.

Do not be a sycophant. No-one will be impressed, not even the target of your attentions.

Do not run, unless you are playing a sport, exercising or there is good reason. Running implies a lack of time, lack of planning or something worse. It can un-nerve the people around you.

Do not contradict your boss in open forum, in a way that undermines their authority or judgement. When contributing to a conversation or debate, be mindful of the power of asking questions over simply expressing your opinions. If you believe that your boss is wrong or mis-informed, take care in picking the moment and manner of your approach. Do your research.

Conversations

People feel most engaged when they have a voice and feel that their opinion matters.

Leaders should exercise intellectual humility. Take care to listen to others, whatever their level of knowledge and intellect. Do not overtly try to impress people with your knowledge and intellect. Enable all people to have a voice.

Be sincere. People will know when consultation is insincere.

Effective conversations can unlock knowledge within a group.

The sharing of opinions and views needs to be civil and constructive for potential conflict to be drawn out and defused, rather than avoided or suppressed.

The key to effective conversations, consultation and debate is clarity. People should be able to express their opinions and views, without fear of judgement. People should be encouraged to explain the reasoning behind their thoughts.

Opinions and comment are most valuable when the provenance is clear. Conversations will be less effective when people are expressing opinions without explaining the context and background behind those views.

Encourage people to be open about the level of objectivity and subjectivity in their views. It is important to know the level of subjectivity being used.

When you offer an opinion or view, explain your reasoning.

When someone offers an opinion, really listen and try to understand what is behind it. Ask as many questions as you can in order to understand the source, motivation, assumptions and reasoning behind the view being expressed. Such an approach has the following benefits:

➢ If the opinion was not well founded, the person may quietly withdraw their opinion without a debate or argument

➢ If you decide that you disagree with their view, your response will be well founded

➢ If you realise that you agree with their view, you will have avoided the potential embarrassment of a hasty response

Expectations

If it looks right, it probably is.

Do not allow yourself to be defined by the past. Use it as something to build from.

Do not expect too much. Understand the capabilities of people. Do not over tax or stretch people unnecessarily.

Good enough may be good enough.

Be conscious of how your actions will be interpreted by others and the consequences of those interpretations - intended and unintended.

There will always be exceptions. Be conscious of those exceptions but do not be driven by them.

People should look the part.

Develop a culture where people want to look the part.

When you visit people and places, approach them with a 'light touch'. Using a manner that is too direct will generate defensive reactions and information will remain hidden. Identify issues that need attention and address them through a follow-up. In this way, people will approach your visits with an open, engaging and productive mind-set.

The standard that you let go and walk past, is the standard you are setting. The key is to choose the right time, place and method for dealing with any issues you have identified.

When making formal inspections/audits/checks/tests, ensure people have had the opportunity to understand the expected standard and the time to achieve it. Identify any issues and shortfalls. Agree the method and timeframe for addressing any issues. Follow-up, monitor and review the closing of any issues.

Most achievements come through a process of trial and error. Expect mistakes. Plan for them and have ways of minimising their impact.

CHAPTER 4

Context

Leaders must understand the past,
have a plan for the way ahead
and reflect on the future

No plan survives contact with reality

Know the world around you

Planning to adapt must be part of the plan

A Reflection on Context

Leadership is fundamentally about keeping your head up and eyes on the horizon, when the here-and-now is trying to hold your attention down in the detail. Leaders need to keep one eye on the wider context and one eye on the present. This was precisely the challenge I faced as commander of 12 (Air Support) Engineer Brigade.

I arrived in the Cambridgeshire town of Waterbeach to take over command of the British Army's only brigade of engineers capable of building and maintaining airfields for the Royal Air Force and the Army's helicopter forces, at home and overseas.

At that time, the task we faced was intense and unprecedented. At the heart of the brigade, we were required by the Ministry of Defence to maintain a squadron of Royal Engineers (100 men and women) at 24 hours notice-to-move. Within a day of being notified, they had to be capable of flying or sailing to anywhere in the world, trained and equipped for the primary role of building airfields, yet capable of facing any task in any setting. Preparing a squadron for such a commitment involved a significant programme of training, equipment preparation and logistical planning. Holding a squadron at that notice-to-move, with every person available and every piece of equipment serviceable, required constant attention and vigilance. While one squadron was held at high readiness, the next squadron was being prepared. To top it all, the whole of the brigade had to be capable of deploying with only 10 days notice.

The high readiness forces were on standby for un-foreseen events. In addition, the brigade was assigned commitments to the UK's current operations overseas. Over the course of a year, the brigade deployed troops on 18 separate occasions to operations in Afghanistan. Those deployments were designed to support the intense air activity on the airfields in Kandahar and Camp Bastion. Over the same period, the brigade deployed troops overseas on 40 other occasions. Those deployments included the building of an airfield in Kenya, the construction of a new airbase in Oman, the repair of the harbour on the island of Tristan Da Cunha following a storm and support to Royal Air Force operations on the Falkland Islands.

Despite all of this frenetic operational activity overseas, there was a good deal of routine business at home. An additional regular regiment was being added to the brigade in order to help with the operational demands and a lot of work was needed to prepare for their arrival. The brigade included 2 reserve regiments, 1 based in Scotland and 1 based in the Midlands. Keeping those regiments recruited, equipped and trained required constant attention. The wider Defence budget was under financial pressure and there was a continual battle to ensure that our soldier's service houses were well maintained, the vehicles and equipment were serviceable and there were sufficient civilian guards for the security checkpoints around the barracks. To top it all, a flu pandemic arrived in the UK in 2009 and the brigade had to make urgent preparations to control access to the barracks, care for the families and support the local civilian community.

Through all of the pressure and intensity, the fundamental challenge was to remember to keep looking ahead, in order to be prepared for what may be coming our way. If we allowed our attention to be entirely fixed on the immediate challenges in front of us, each new task would have been a surprise and we would have always been struggling to deal with the latest priority. By taking regular time to look ahead, we were able to plan and be better prepared for the potential challenges ahead.

How did we remember to keep lifting our thoughts and attention? First and foremost, we articulated an ethos that would act as a continuous reminder.

After some debate and consideration, we adopted a simple headline philosophy:

"Ready for anything"

This 'philosophy', as we called it, served as a living reminder that we needed to deliver our current tasks whilst thinking about and preparing for the future, both known and unknown. We used this headline in all of our meetings, plans and presentations.

As reinforcement to this philosophy, we held workshops for the leadership teams at all levels on subjects that would encourage them to think laterally and monitor the wider context. Those workshops included creative thinking, planning methods, horizon scanning, risk analysis and brainstorming techniques.

We commissioned a competition to write a poem about 'The Air Support Engineer'. The judging criteria included recognition for the diverse nature of the role. We commissioned a competition to select an emblem. The brigade had a number (12) but did not have an emblem - common amongst brigades in the British Army. We selected the Osprey Sea Hawk, to reflect the ability of the brigade to go anywhere - land, sea and air.

Perhaps most importantly, despite the frenetic pace of events, we were resolute in our determination to protect a vibrant social programme for the soldiers and their families, in order to give everyone space to relax and reflect.

The here-and-now can feel all consuming, with no time for wider reflection or planning. However, our actions are always within a wider context. The more time leaders take to reflect, think and plan, the more they will be in control of the present.

Context

Your ability to deliver, adapt and improve will be dependent on how well you have understood your context:

Time
Challengers, Opponents
Geography, Location
History, Legacy
Logistics, Resources
People
Policies, Priorities
Stakeholders, Customers, Interest Groups
Unforeseen, Unimagined

The more deeply you consider the potential scenarios and events that may occur in the future (positive and adverse), the more effective and efficient you will be in responding to them.

Take care when judging how much effort to put into testing potential scenarios - not enough and you may be caught out, too much and you could be paralysed by the scale of analysis.

Think carefully about how to set up the testing of potential scenarios - when, how, whom. Keep it under review. Be flexible, in order to match the tempo of real world events.

Time

Keep watching the clock.

Timing is everything - take time, to pick the right time.

You must know and manage your own time before you can manage the time of others.

Make regular time (and protect it) to think and plan. Pick the time of day when your mind is clear and able to think freely. Remove any distractions.

A perfect plan, delivered too early or too late, will be a partial or complete failure.

Leaders must think in terms of near and far. Short term priorities and activities should fit within a sustainable long term programme.

In your forward planning, be conscious of the need for a rhythm that delivers periods of recuperation between periods of higher tempo.

Think carefully about when to change gear, from steady state to high tempo, and back.

Be ready to act quickly and decisively, when needed.

Do not act in haste.

Each day, use a prioritised list of what you must do that day. Draw a distinction between the important and minor things that need to be done that day. Discard the note at the end of the day, and prepare a new one for the next day.

Maintain a prioritised list of long term tasks covering urgent and routine, drawing a distinction between the important ones and the minor ones.

Attend meetings, events and activities where your attendance will have some value. Avoid attending for attendance sake.

Do not add something new at short notice, unless there are genuine benefits to be gained and value added.

Planned short notice changes should fit the intended purpose and desired outcome. If you must make short notice changes, explain the background and the purpose.

Do not accept a culture or habit of short notice changes, borne out of weaknesses in planning. When necessary, short notice changes should be formally considered and enacted.

Location

Leaders must think long and wide.

Do not be constrained by what is directly in front of you.

Know the immediate place around you in detail.

Consider how much detail you need to know about the more distant places ahead, to the sides and behind you.

Never stop thinking about what is over the horizon.

Information

First reports are often inaccurate.

Work hard to establish the facts, before making a decision.

If you make an assessment based on incomplete information, make sure people know the limitations of that assessment. As the assessment improves, update people on progress.

Rushing to judgement often leads to 'chasing the error': an inaccurate assessment leads to a flawed response, an adjustment tries to put the error right, but fails in part, further adjustments try again ... and so on.

If you make a hasty judgement that proves to be partially inaccurate, it is often best to go back and re-set from the starting point, rather than adjust from the point of inaccuracy.

Leaders need two types of information source:

Formal - Input from formal sources.

Informal - Input from sources who will tell you how it really is, rather than what they think you want to hear.

As a leader, you must keep all news (good and bad) in perspective.

Good news tends to travel up communication channels more quickly than bad news.

Bad news is received badly when it is found to have been delayed or hidden. Giving early warning often mitigates most of the potential negative impact of bad news.

If you are not hearing complaints and gripes, they are probably going un-reported. Go and find them.

Silence is not necessarily good news.

You must understand the authenticity and accuracy of information you are being offered, otherwise it is just noise.

'Press to Test' - use open questions to draw out the level of validity and understanding behind information.

If a straight question receives a straight answer, then it is probably safe to move on.

If an answer does not address the question, then it is worth exploring the issue in more detail.

Too much data can overwhelm - paralysis by analysis.

Too much explicit instruction can overload and inhibit people.

When offering information to others, ensure you articulate the level of objectivity and/or subjectivity involved.

In the long term, people will come to trust and value your views if they understand the validity of the information and how much subjective opinion has been used.

Stakeholders

Leaders must invest in those around them - above, beside and below.

Often, the most important stakeholder in your success is your boss. If you need to improve the relationship, take action. It is up to you to make the change for the better.

Leadership is as much about taking your boss and your peer group along with you, as it is about leading your team.

Understand that engagement develops in clusters. The greatest impact on those clusters is from the leaders and influencers within those clusters.

If your purpose and objectives involve serving customers (internal and external), do not just focus on finding out what they want, put them at the core of everything you do.

Key stakeholders should be included in planning processes, unless otherwise specified, security dictates or time is short.

Key stakeholders should feel that they part-own the decisions.

In order to influence someone, you must understand their nature, world-view, levels of formality, emotional reactions, ambitions and their context (background, agenda, environment, constraints).

In seeking to influence large groups of people, identify the target groups (movers, shakers, stakeholders), simple core messages, timelines and the responses you are trying to generate. Look to build momentum in the influence and engagement you are bringing to bear on the target groups.

When engaging and influencing stakeholders, avoid jargon, use evidence and stories, be positive and upbeat, use memorable quotes and anticipate potentially awkward questions.

CHAPTER 5

Leading

Everyone leads

Everyone influences

Some deliberately, some un-knowingly

Some welcome it, some shun it

Embrace it

A Reflection on Leading

The British Army has a way of throwing you in at the deep end. Fortunately, it provides you with exceptional training and life experiences, as well as support from some of the finest people to ever walk on this earth, otherwise known as Non-Commissioned Officers. They are the corporals, sergeants and warrant officers who work alongside the commissioned officers (trained at the Royal Military Academy Sandhurst and received a commission from the reigning monarch).

After completing the officer training at Sandhurst and the engineer officer training at the Royal School of Military Engineering, I was posted to Nienburg in Germany. The Cold War was still alive and kicking. I had no sense that this posting would be a warm up for the daunting leadership challenge that would come next. I set about putting the Sandhurst leadership theory into practice. At that time, the British Army on the Rhine was tasked with defending Western Europe from a potential assault by hordes of Soviet tanks and shock troops. At least 3 or 4 times a year, we would be called out of barracks with less than 6 hours' notice. When the siren sounded, we had to grab everyone we could find, load the armoured personnel carriers and engineer tanks, drive to tactical holding areas in nearby woods, receive orders and then complete engineer tasks designed to block thousands of Soviet tanks.

It was a surreal period. The threat from the Soviet Union still felt very real and the local West German population put up with all sorts of inconvenience and disruption. They were very supportive of the allied armies encamped in their neighbourhoods, drinking in their bars and driving across their fields. We regularly drove columns of heavy armoured engineer tanks on the German roads, created clouds of smoke, woke up neighbourhoods, tore up pavements with the tank tracks, made camps in farm buildings and drove over farm crops in simulated battles. In preparation for the potential attack from the Soviet Union, we practiced laying minefields across the German countryside (with practice anti-tank mines made of cardboard and sand). We rehearsed placing demolition charges on the big steel bridges that crossed the German rivers and canals. Although inert, the practice demolition charges were very heavy. One fell off a bridge during an exercise and created an instant sunroof in a passing car (thankfully, without hurting the driver).

Three months after I left that posting in Germany, the Berlin Wall came down.

My 2 years in Germany passed by in a flash. It felt like I had only just begun to learn how to put leadership theory into practice. I quickly realised that the leadership heat had been turned up a few notches. I found myself out of the frying pan and in the proverbial fire. I had passed the Commando Course after completing officer training at Sandhurst and before the posting to Germany. On the strength of my Commando qualification, I was posted from Germany to the commando bomb disposal troop based in Kent. There I met Sergeant 'Stan' Dean and Corporal 'Archie' Gaunt. I slowly came to realise that they would provide me with the sort of support that many leaders can only dream of.

Each year, the troop deployed to Norway with the Royal Marine-led 3 Commando Brigade for 3 months of winter warfare training. We undertook the winter warfare courses, trained alongside the commando engineer squadron and practised the art of bomb disposal in arctic conditions. The culmination of the 3 month deployment was always a large scale naval exercise which included amphibious landings on Norwegian beaches, fighting a mock-enemy consisting of Norwegian Special Forces and regular troops. Sergeant Dean and Corporal Gaunt were my right arm, my backbone and often my frontal lobe. They were that essential mix of practical experience, positive critique and reliable implementation. They were utterly loyal and supportive, but by no means 'yes men'. I sought their counsel and advice at every turn. They rewarded me with advice that was direct, honest, at times hard to take, always positive and steadfastly professional. Once we had conferred and debated, I would take the decisions and they would stand shoulder-to-shoulder alongside me. We were united as a leadership team, able to face the commando engineers we led and the Royal Marines we supported.

Back in the United Kingdom, we trained as 'high risk' searchers and bomb disposal operators. In time of war, our role was to search for terrorist bombs. Once found, our task was to disarm or dispose of those devices. At that time, the 'Troubles' in Northern Ireland were still in full swing and we completed the training courses that were designed for troops deploying to that war-torn Province. We trained hard. As commando bomb disposal engineers, we nurtured a distinct team identity based around excellence, professionalism, servant leadership, comradeship, a train-hard-fight-easy approach and a collective determination to live up to the example set by our commando forebears. We took every opportunity to socialise as hard as we trained. We were a band of brothers fused through the bonds of commando training, commando history and the intensity of our bomb disposal role.

There was always one activity that got my blood pumping harder than any other. We provided support to the UK's maritime Special Forces group. The group was responsible for the defence of the UKs off-shore maritime interests. Simply put, they protected the nation's ships and oil/gas platforms. They were the best. The group held monthly exercises in various locations around the UK coast. They would be based in an aircraft hangar and flown out to the target ship or platform. However, they did not have expertise in 'high risk' search - looking for terrorist bombs. That was where we came in. We would deploy as part of the assault wave and look for explosive devices that may have been placed around the ship or platform. These were the times when I truly relied on Sergeant Dean and Corporal Gaunt.

One dark stormy night over the North Sea, I was in the belly of a Chinook helicopter heading towards an oil platform in the assault wave of an exercise. I was feeling the pressure. The Special Forces operators were welcoming, professional and good humoured. However, they were intimidating to be around, due to the power of the energy they exuded - their resolve and determination.

Standing bunched up in the darkened belly of a Chinook helicopter was exhilarating and terrifying. Corporal Gaunt was directly behind me and Sergeant Dean was following in the next helicopter. The pilot was an experienced Special Forces pilot but the ride still felt like a roll-a-coaster. We all knew the task that the pilot faced. He had to hover in a strong cross wind, 120 feet above the foaming sea, in order to hold the helicopter's position over a landing pad that was designed for much smaller helicopters. His rotor blades were so wide that he could only drop us at the outer edge of the landing pad.

The internal red lights came on. We had arrived at the platform and the Chinook flared into a hover. Fast-roping involved putting on a pair of rough leather gloves, grabbing hold of the thick rope, descending down the rope and letting go when you reached the bottom. On this occasion the rope was attached to the inside roof of the Chinook and I would be descending down through a dark square hole in the helicopter floor. I waited for my turn and watched the Special Forces assault troops descend down the rope through the black hole. I would be the first of the engineer 'high risk' search team to descend the rope. As I stepped down into the dark hole, I felt burning on my hands from the burning rope, my nostrils filled with aviation exhaust fumes and my eyes burst into life as the darkness of the Chinook was replaced by the bright white lights of the oil platform.

My enthusiasm turned to horror as I came to the end of the rope without reaching the landing pad. I could not stop and braced for the long fall (120 feet) down to the foaming sea. My hands slipped from the end of the rope. Thankfully I fell no more than 6 feet, landing on top of the Special Forces trooper who had descended the rope in front of me and was now tangled in the safety netting at the side of the landing pad. The pilot had been battling the wind and the helicopter had drifted a couple of feet sideways as we descended the rope. Corporal Gaunt was directly behind me. By the time he reached the bottom of the rope, the helicopter had moved back over the landing pad. The safety net was attached to the platform a few feet below the level of the landing pad. Corporal Gaunt stood on the edge of the landing pad, took one look down at me in the net and headed off across the landing pad in the direction of the assault troops.

It took a few minutes to untangle myself from the safety net, climb up on to the helicopter landing pad and catch up with the troop. It was all over by the time I got there. The flight back felt much longer than the flight out, as I contemplated the post-exercise review and the inevitable humiliation of explaining my absence from the assault to the entire assembled Special Forces group.

Back in the hangar, the group commander started the review with an outline resume of the exercise. He explained that he wanted to focus on the issue that had arisen at the landing pad. I wished that the earth would swallow me up. I was not listening closely to him, as I was busy rehearsing the excuses in my head. Slowly, the group commander's words became clearer to me and more distinct. I realised that the whole Special Forces group had turned and was looking at our search team. The look in their eyes was not distain, but the quiet look of admiration that fellow professionals give you when you have done something well. The group commander was explaining how our performance had set a standard. He had watched our preparations closely and our conduct during the assault. As well as our technical preparations, we had built resilience in our team. The Special Forces commander explained to the entire assembled group that I had come off the end of the rope and fallen into the safety net. Corporal Gaunt had realised that it would take too long to get me out of the net. He had done the right thing, left me in the net and quickly re-joined the assault troops. Sergeant Dean had arrived moments later in the following aircraft. Between them, they had calmly taken over, followed the assault troops through the oil platform and successfully found all of the mock terrorist devices. The group commander was delighted and was clearly intent on using the experience as an example for the wider group. Indeed, in many of the following exercises, he adopted the practice of pulling Special Forces team commanders out of the exercises at various stages, in order to test how the remainder of their team would react.

I would like to say that I had foreseen the incident and had understood what needed to be done to prepare for such an eventuality. I had not. However, failure is a powerful learning tool. My personal failure that night (landing in the net and missing most of the action), served to highlight the need to build a strong self-supporting leadership team, train hard under realistic pressure, build strong team bonds professionally and socially, value loyalty and integrity, plan for unlikely eventualities as well as the likely ones, plan to adapt and keep moving forward in the face of adversity.

That night on that oil platform demonstrated the essence of leading a team. The task is to build a team that is capable of performing at the required level, with or without the leader present. Leaders cannot lead on their own. Every leader needs to spend time, resources and energy on developing their equivalent of Sergeant Dean and Corporal Gaunt.

Your Essence

You can feel the pulse of leadership when people are willingly leaning into the organisational spaces and cracks around them, endeavouring to fill them ... rather than sitting back with their heads down and quietly watching the cracks widen.

Aim to make a difference to the lives of the people you lead.

Be yourself. Be authentic.

Leadership is a human endeavour. You may have wise words and personal credibility. You may even be in the right time and place. However, people respond most deeply to emotional connection. Be there, engage, persuade, debate, direct, give thanks, be interested, listen.

People will know your heart. You must believe in what you are doing. People will sense insincerity.

You are working with people, rather than to people.

Awake your passions.

Although you identify with the group, you are not the same, you are the leader.

Leadership is not a popularity contest. It is not about being liked or fitting in. However, it is about being respected. Respect is gained through engaging people, taking an interest in people as individuals, being clear about goals, focussing on performance, fairness, consistency, making decisions and being accountable.

To lead others, you must first understand yourself.

Observe your own feelings, responses and actions.

You have to be honest with yourself, in order to be honest with other people.

Take your own advice. Walk the walk. Be true and consistent.

Take ownership.

Leadership requires courage - physical, moral, emotional.

When courage is required, look beyond the moment in order to judge what is right.

A real leader is driven by conscience and integrity rather than safety, expediency or vanity.

Not all decisions have to be courageous.

Trust is embedded at the heart of leadership - slow to earn and easily lost.

The essence of leadership is letting go - clearly expressing the goals and purpose, setting out the framework (resources, financial, geographical, legal, etc) within which people should act and letting them flourish within it.

In letting go and trusting people, keep a respectful distance, but not too far ..... be in a position to monitor progress so that you are able to provide timely support when it is needed.

Trust is a two-way relationship.

Ensure people understand that trust is a judgement, something to be earned and sustained - not a right to be expected.

Be as accurate as you can be. Do not make it up. Be clear and open about how sure you are, or not. You may get away with the occasional pretence, but potentially at the expense of long term trust in you.

If in doubt, ask for direction. Do not guess when further guidance may be available.

Speak and act coherently. Follow up your words with the promised deeds or explain what has changed.

Manners are everything.

Be compassionate, especially when you have to be decisive and make difficult decisions.

You Leading

Leadership is a craft, a mix of science and art.

Through all the pressures and conflicting demands of life, pay close attention to maintaining balance and structure in your leadership. Leaders must sustain an appropriate balance in the time and energy they apply to understanding, listening, reviewing, adjusting, directing, instructing, encouraging, persuading and explaining.

As a general guide, aim to spend ¼ of your time understanding and listening, ¼ of your time reviewing and directing, and ½ of your time engaging, explaining and encouraging.

A key indicator of effective leadership is found in the vitality of the relationship between the leader and their team, combined with the clarity of understanding between them about the strategy, objectives and intended plan.

The first and last task of leadership is to provide clarity around the goal and purpose, and to maintain that focus ... relentlessly.

The more people you involve in the development of strategy, the more likely it is to engage people, drive the organisation and provide an effective long term framework for action.

People are reliant on you to be the thinker - make enough regular time to pause, reflect and think.

Silence is a place of inspiration.

The more you think, the less others sweat and toil.

Be clear about what you are trying to achieve.

You must be clear with yourself before you can be clear with others. Clarity is first and last.

Answer the question 'Why are we here?'

If you think you've worked hard enough at explaining the goal and purpose, keep going.

Goals and objectives should have longevity and not change too often.

Avoid setting people more than 5 objectives at any one time.

Prioritise, prioritise, prioritise. Regularly review and update priorities.

Leaders set the standard through their words, actions, manner, humour, attitude and demeanour.

Learn from others, but be yourself. People are un-nerved by leaders who appear to be trying to emulate someone else.

Recognise and understand the source of your position as leader. Understand where your leadership authority is coming from. It may be from one or more of the following sources:

- ➤ Your personality, character and personal identity
- ➤ Your energy, commitment and resilience
- ➤ Your formal position in an organisation or group
- ➤ Your expertise, knowledge and experience
- ➤ Your ability to reward or punish
- ➤ Your network and ability to influence stakeholders

One of the key leadership skills is to judge when to be closely involved and when to step back. At times, you may need to lead by example and get closely involved in directing from the front. But, always remember your primary role of thinking ahead. You will not have the time and space to think if you are too close, too often.

Maintain an appropriate and respectful distance in your professional relationships. Too much distance and you may appear arrogant or dis-engaged. Too close and you may lack the authority to lead in the difficult moments.

Be mindful of your potential impact on others. People will be watching your actions and listening to your words. Be conscious of how your actions and words may be interpreted by others, intended and unintended.

Treat people fairly and consistently.

Do not have favourites, do not be seen to have favourites.

Be consistent. Acting inconsistently saps people's confidence and respect.

People need to feel that you are accessible to them.

Make written notes of issues and problems, to stop them obstructing your thinking.

If you find yourself overwhelmed or uncertain, then pause, step back, reflect and consider, before moving on.

You must be capable of pushing back on things you have been told to do, when appropriate. Of course you must look upwards to your boss, take care of your own needs and deliver on the goals that have been set for you. But there is a balance. Everyone around you, above and below, will be impressed if you make a stand when the time, place and cause are right.

Pick your battles with your boss ... too often and you will become a noise to be ignored ... too little and you will not carry the authority to be listened to.

Be kind to yourself, everyone has room to grow.

Decision Making

Ensure that you have a balancing voice, a foil, a counter view, a sounding board, in order to balance your decision making.

Do not assume that you always know more than others.

A good test of decision making - if someone did it to you, would you consider it to be fair and reasonable?

Create formal and informal ways for you and your team to explore potential viewpoints, consider options and encourage creative thought.

Look for the unknown knowns within the team. Someone may well have the answer.

Watch out for constrained, inhibited and compliant thinking.

Decisions are not always simple choices between right and wrong. When you face a tricky dilemma, the best you can do may be to make a judgement around the most appropriate balance. Identify the 'least worst' way forward.

Formal deliberate decision making involves:

- Clearly stated goals, aims and objectives
- Clearly stated specific tasks
- Clarity around freedoms and constraints
- Identification of available resources
- Time to research
- Examination of the options, including the 'most likely' and the 'worst case'
- Clarification and confirmation - to avoid errors in translation or mis-understandings
- Decision(s)
- Communication of the decision(s)
- Support and respect for the decision(s)
- Decision(s) turned into action
- Clearly stated responsibilities for implementation
- Co-ordination between decision makers
- Monitoring progress, to respond quickly and effectively

When time is short, use as much of the formal decision making tools as possible - do not just wing it.

Experimentation should aim to draw out the potential options.

Ensure people know how much authority they have to exploit an opportunity, to improvise, and how to secure approval if higher authority is required.

People must know what authority they have to choose to do or not to do something.

People must know what authority they have to stop others doing something.

Rules, processes and procedures should feel like a lifejacket rather than a straitjacket.

People should be accountable for their results and outcomes.

Be prepared in detail for the most likely outcome.

Consider the worst case potential outcome and your potential responses.

Choosing not to do something can be a valid decision.

Avoidance is not a true option, as it may catch up with you, to your detriment. If you must avoid a decision, ensure that you have a strategy for dealing with the effects.

Find ways to seek out genuine critical feedback on your decision making, without undermining your position and authority.

It is better to think through feedback, than fight through it. Think through any feedback and decide whether to act upon it.

Whether giving or receiving feedback, remember that criticism is not always reasonable, fair, accurate or justified.

Listen most attentively to criticism coming from people whose judgement you value.

If you must disagree with someone, explain where you are coming from, how you reached your view and the reasons behind it. You should consider offering your thoughts on the way forward.

Develop people to make their own decisions. Do not interfere in the detail of people's planning and decision making, unless you really need to.

If you are making a decision in writing, reflect on whether you would be content for the decision to become public.

Adapting

Being prepared, and able, to adapt must be part of the plan.

Styles of leadership are sometimes described as if they are coats to be put on and off. However, the real world does not work in straight lines.

You must be capable of employing different leadership styles sequentially or simultaneously, as required.

In adapting your leadership, match your approach to the:

➢ People in front of you
➢ Boss above you
➢ Stakeholders around you
➢ Task ahead
➢ Time available
➢ Place
➢ Resources available to you

There will be times when you will need to dive in and manage the detail, but this should not be routine.

Leaders must apply the majority of their energies to thinking ahead, engaging, inspiring, supporting and reinforcing.

Leadership styles occupy a broad spectrum. In considering your approach, be mindful of the following styles:

Lighthouse   Illuminates the way ahead
Articulates the goal and purpose
Encourages people to find the way forward

Requires courage and trust
Needs regular re-stating of the goal

Supportive   Sets people off in the right direction
Gives people freedom and space to work
Offers guidance, training and support
Monitors progress
When needed, picks people up and re-sets them

Requires investment in time and effort
Generates long term organic growth
Builds resilience

Grass-cutter   Goes ahead - physically or figuratively
Helicopter   Cuts a path for people to follow
Constantly present - physically or figuratively
Directs people what to do and when to do it

Generates action when time is short, when trust
is low and/or there has been limited training
Generates an instant response
Does not build self-reliance or resilience

Adapt, adjust, change - do whatever it takes to keep moving forward, keep or regain the momentum, and stay ahead.

Keep an open mind - look for opportunities.

Continuously monitor, review, seek out information and prepare for what may come next.

When there are a number of challenges to be addressed, deal with the most immediate source of dislocation, discomfort or threat.

Communicating

The best path to the brain runs through the heart.

Without effective communication, you are relying on osmosis for information to be passed.

Find ways to touch people's hearts. Tell them something authentic. Show them what you are passionate about.

Use stories to help define who you are. Define yourself before others define you.

Use stories to engage people - explain who 'we' are and what 'we' are going to do.

Stories need to be authentic, otherwise they will lose their power and may become a negative.

You must live up to the stories you tell.

Be accessible to people. Look for opportunities to reinforce your message and receive feedback.

Programme time to get out and visit people where they work. Better still, work alongside them from time to time. Protect that time. It will bring you real insight.

Be engaging, open and candid.

Listening can be a powerful means of communicating.

Use as many channels as possible and keep repeating your message.

People readily pick up strong visual messages.

Never assume that people have understood what you have told them. Not everyone will have heard it. There will be different interpretations of what you said. Check how it has been interpreted. Tell them again. Check again.

Drop your voice when making a key point, and pause for people to recognise the significance.

Engage people and magnify your messages through a network of messengers:

➢ Find credible people to act as messengers, whether volunteers or selected
➢ Messengers should be knowledgeable, persuasive and in the right place
➢ Keep the messengers informed
➢ Provide the time and resources for messengers to lead workplace conversations
➢ Provide stories to give the messages resonance

The most effective messages are simple and memorable.

Messages that engage people emotionally will self-generate and expand through people.

Make sure that you talk the same language as the people you are leading. Be on the same planet. Avoid jargon.

Communication must reinforce the organisation. Take care not to leave people out or bypass them.

Communication must be two-way.

Monitor what is going on. For you to make timely decisions and adjustments, you need to have an overview of activity and progress. It does not imply a lack of trust. The balance between empowering and trusting people, versus maintaining your awareness and readiness to respond, requires constant judgement and adjustment.

Know and monitor the detail, but avoid meddling in the detailed business of others. Dive into the detail when someone is struggling and needs support, to learn a lesson or to reinforce success. Step back from the detail when you are able.

Create the conditions for people to feel open to seeking clarification when they need it.

Do not talk across people.

Add value to communications, do not just be a post box.

Failures in communication flows, resistance to change and general scepticism are often found in the middle of a team.

Develop ways to monitor the effectiveness of information flows.

You cannot lead mushrooms - kept in the dark and fed on organic matter. There may be valid short term benefits or good reasons for holding back, restricting access to information and managing the release of information. However, routinely keeping people in the dark may lead to them keeping their heads down and doing the minimum to get by.

Keeping people in the dark, because it's easier that way, is not leadership.

CHAPTER 6

People

You must be able to lead the people in front of you

*People come in all forms, personalities, intellects,
characters and motivations*

You are at your best when you bring out the best in others

Leaders engage people - all of the people

A Reflection on People

I received a formal letter with the news that I had been selected for the rank of Brigadier and would be posted to the Defence Infrastructure Organisation as Head of the Defence Training Estate and International. I would be responsible for the UK Ministry of Defence training facilities and estate across the UK - 1% of the rural UK (157,000 ha), 120+ training facilities, 8100+ buildings and 3500+ kilometres of roads. I would also be responsible for the UK Ministry of Defence bases in Belize, Canada, Cyprus, Germany, Gibraltar, Kenya, Nepal and the South Atlantic.

I was thrilled and excited. At that stage, I did not fully appreciate that I would be responsible for 245 military staff, 110 civil servants, 1850 contractors and 780 local overseas staff. I certainly had no idea that I would be leading those dispersed worldwide teams through a dramatic transformation programme.

I arrived at my office in Warminster feeling positive, energised and elated. The office seemed to be full of professional, experienced and committed people, with a focus on the primary output - training troops for military operations. My personal assistant, Beverley Thomas, was a kind hearted woman from South Wales. She seemed to epitomise the spirit in the office. Despite being paid a relatively modest salary, she was eternally positive, flexible and prepared to work beyond her contracted hours to get the job done.

On my third day in the job, I was invited to a hotel in the Midlands for a workshop with all of the Defence Infrastructure Organisation senior executives. Something big was brewing.

The Ministry of Defence had recruited a Chief Executive Officer from an external commercial role. I liked him and we got on well. However, the scale of what was to come soon became apparent. The Ministry of Defence had decided that the defence infrastructure operating budget (people) would be cut by over 50% and the delivery budget (contracted services) would be cut by over 30%. We would be losing over half of our direct workforce. The Defence estate would be reduced in size. A large team of consultants had been employed to assist with designing the revised organisation, developing new ways of working, running the change programme and rationalising the estate.

I returned to Warminster in a very different mood. Our teams were flat out supporting the training of troops for military operations in Afghanistan and Iraq. I was not sure how we would have time to deliver the transformation programme. I was particularly concerned about the effect on the morale, motivation and commitment of our people, at a time when they should be focussed on preparing troops for military operations. I did not know how to go about telling Beverley and the rest of the team.

Over the following weeks, the scale of the transformation programme became even more daunting. We would be competing all of the prime contracts, through which we delivered facilities services and range safety management to our end users. The procurement programme would be a major undertaking, taking at least 2 years to deliver an outcome. At the same time, the Defence Infrastructure Organisation would be recruiting a Strategic Business Partner. This partner would recruit senior executives from the external commercial world to work alongside the senior civil servants and military officers, to deliver the required budget savings and estate rationalisation.

I asked Beverley to arrange a gathering of our regional managers from across the UK and our overseas bases, for a 3-day workshop on the way ahead. We gathered in a World War 2 vintage hut in the middle of the Salisbury Plain military training area. I had picked the location to keep us grounded in our fundamental role of training troops for combat operations. With artillery shells exploding on a nearby artillery firing range, we sat down to consider the way ahead.

There was no point pulling any punches. I laid it out as honestly and openly as I could and waited for the wave of angry responses. There was a palpable sense of hurt in the group that we would have to go through a transformation programme while preparing troops for combat operations. However, what came through at the heart of their responses was not entirely expected.

The group quickly started to think about solutions and the way forward. The answer was going to be our people. The group debated a set of principles that we would all embrace to see our teams through the transformation programme. As leaders, we would be honest, open and available at all times to our staff. We would work hard to engage our staff, to listen and modify our plans when appropriate. I watched Beverley as she took the notes at the back of the room. Her face had been full of trepidation and uncertainty. By lunchtime on the first day, her face was relaxed, calm and smiling. I knew we were heading in the right direction.

I had gone into the workshop thinking that we may get bogged down in feelings of hurt and negativity. Instead, I was gripped with a growing sense of admiration and pride. This group of leaders had travelled from far and wide to meet in a draughty wooden hut in the Wiltshire countryside and had been faced with a stark presentation about the transformation challenge head. Instead of throwing their hands up in horror, they had set about thinking through the way ahead. Rather than revising organisation charts and debating how to carve up the reduced budget, they were focussed on the need to keep our people at the heart of the transformation process.

As leaders, they recognised the need to step up and lead the transformation rather than resist it. We were a widely dispersed organisation with many different cultures and world-views. Our teams stretched from Salisbury Plain in Wiltshire to Belfast in Northern Ireland, Sennybridge in Wales, Dartmoor in Devon,

Hythe in Kent, Thetford in East Anglia, Alberta in Canada, Nanyuki in Kenya, Kathmandu in Nepal, and to Gibraltar.

As well as committing to a set of principles for leading our people through the transformation, we agreed a rhythm of staff engagement activities that would include 'town hall' open meetings, structured conversations, workshops, blogs and team development activities.

Most significantly, we began the practice of working alongside staff. As part of the programme of visits by senior leaders to the regional teams, we included time to work alongside staff. I found myself manning a call centre switchboard, driving across the Kenyan countryside as a range warden and checking safety equipment near Belfast as a safety marshal. Those working visits were often the most productive in terms of hearing what people really thought.

When the big day came and the Strategic Business Partner arrived, with all of the changes to our ways of working, I embarked on a 5-week roadshow around the UK and overseas. I was determined to place myself in front of every member of staff around the world, to explain what was happening, to listen to their views and to answer their questions. I came back impressed by the open and positive reception from all of the teams.

There was still a good deal of work to be done. When I left the role 4 years later, the transformation programme was still going and our regional managers were still working hard to keep their staff engaged within the new organisation, budgets and ways of working.

Through 4 years of transformation, we had kept the military training going without any failing on our part. During that period, we did not receive a single formal complaint from end users attributable to our services and management. The annual customer satisfaction level did not fall below 93% in the surveys that were completed by every user of the training facilities. Our teams scored 7% points above the 'high performing team' benchmark in the Ministry of Defence annual staff engagement surveys.

What saw us through was leadership, at every level. Our leadership teams recognised the need to lead the transformation rather than resist it. There were some very difficult days and lots of bumps along the way. However, we got through by keeping our people at the heart of our plans. They responded with patience, understanding and commitment.

People

Leadership is not a question with an answer, nor a journey with a destination.

Leadership must adapt and adjust to work with the people in that time and place.

One size does not fit all.

No two leaders are the same.

No two groups of people are the same.

The people around you will change and develop over time.

Individuals may change their attitude, approach, motivations and responses between places and situations.

Groups change and develop as individuals join and leave.

Individuals

Build the individuals and the team will follow.

Invest in the development of people. That investment will be your main legacy when you are gone.

Know people as individuals - when they are happy, when they are down, what makes them bored, what fires them up, what makes them tick. Keep in touch with them.

People are looking for a challenging, busy and rewarding life that gives them purpose, self-esteem and dignity.

Set the conditions for people to flourish.

People will feel most engaged if:

➢ They receive recognition or praise for good work
➢ They know what is expected of them
➢ They have friends at work
➢ They make a positive contribution to the stated goal

Say 'thank you', as often as it is deserved. It is a powerful motivator. Be enthusiastic in saying it.

Ensure that people feel connected to the goal and objectives, by understanding their own role and contribution.

People respond positively when:

- ➢ They have the materials and equipment to do the job
- ➢ They feel cared about as a person
- ➢ Their development and learning is encouraged
- ➢ Their opinions seem to count
- ➢ The people around them are committed to quality

Positive and productive working relationships have a significant impact on attitudes and motivations.

Encourage work colleagues to be friends.

Ensure people understand the legacy that they should leave.

Individuals have bio-rhythms. You cannot keep people at a peak all of the time. Leaders shape the rhythm of the team. Build the team to peaks of performance and throttle back in between.

If you put people under pressure, understand the response that you may generate within them - flight, fight, freeze. Be mindful of the way you intend to manage their responses.

Manage people's emotional and stress responses through explaining, listening, distractions, rewards and recognition.

People are not able to handle excessive prolonged stress. Manage people and teams as organic systems that have cycles and rhythms.

The reaction to stress can become a positive response to be harnessed rather than a harmful reaction to be avoided.

Encourage people to walk towards a challenge, embrace it and enjoy the anticipation of achievement.

Individuals can be taught to think under stress and pressure. They must understand the steps in the process that lead to the required outcome. The steps should be practised and rehearsed to the point where the process takes care of itself without the need for deliberate thought.

Practice builds confidence.

Building momentum is about building a rhythm.

Practice should build in intensity towards the required level.

You can tell when individuals are dis-engaged, as they keep their head down and lean away from challenges. When people are positively engaged, they will keep their head up, look around and lean into challenges without being asked.

Teams

Teams have always been at the heart of human achievement.

You can feel the pulse of an effective team - the energy, vitality and activity are largely self-generating ... without having to rely on regular instruction and direction.

Highly effective and efficient teams are brought together by inspiring and engaging leaders.

A group of people is not necessarily a team. A team is a group of people who are interconnected and interdependent (to some extent), and focussed towards a goal that can only be achieved through their collective efforts.

Team leadership starts by defining the team - what it stands for and its purpose.

Teams need leaders to define their purpose, take decisions and model appropriate behaviours.

Goals should cause excitement.

The challenge is to keep everyone aligned to the goal and objectives, while allowing individuals and teams to express themselves and flourish.

People may feel that they do not inherently like working in teams, but every significant goal needs a team to achieve it. The ability for people to take their place in a team is an essential skill.

Leadership should be shared and not seen as something done by the top.

When you introduce yourself to a group of 10 people, 2 or 3 may really like you (whatever you do), 2 or 3 may not like you (whatever you do), and the others may take you as they find you. Accept it. Work with it.

The most effective teams are clear about what is expected to be part of that team:

- ➢ Commitment and values
- ➢ Energy and effort
- ➢ Mind-set and behaviour
- ➢ Language
- ➢ Communication
- ➢ Debate and challenge
- ➢ Learning and development, including induction

Values define who we are as individuals and as teams.

Values should be aspirational, providing clarity for everyone.

When values are expressed and observed, they can form the basis of trust. Even if they are not openly declared, they may be inferred from wider activity and behaviour.

If expressed, values must be enduring and not subject to frequent change.

If you seek to change the values or adjourn from them when you come under pressure, then they are probably wrong - or you are.

There is little point expressing values unless you live and work by them, they are seen and heard, they form the basis for performance management and they are explored through discussion and debate. Trust is easily lost when values become ignored or discredited.

Teams should strive to have members with the appropriate range of skills, knowledge and experience for the task, whilst recognising the need for future growth and flexibility.

People are fundamentally social beings who try to find meaning.

The most significant impact on people comes from the group dynamic, which can be positive (reinforcing) or negative (diminishing). The primary leadership aim must be to foster a positive identity, energy and social vitality within the team.

Social vitality is the social energy between people. It is built through the social interaction that people experience within their job roles, beyond their immediate role and in wider social settings. It is reflected in the level of helpfulness, trust, loyalty and empathy within a group. Social vitality takes time to build and needs the attention of leaders to nurture it.

Find ways for people to get to know each other beyond their immediate role and place.

Make time for people to engage with each other socially.

Every voice should be heard within a team. Ensure that the loudest voices do not dominate and that the quietest voices are heard. Make the time and space for all voices to be heard.

Everyone should know how to find help.

Identity comes from meaningful distinctiveness that is enduring and not transient.

People have individual identities and multiple social identities. People are adept at switching their performance and behaviour between social settings and identities.

Foster a positive group identity around the task in-hand, to the point that it becomes self-reinforcing. Allow the narrative around the identity to evolve.

Most organisations will be strengthened by the development of distinct identities at different levels, within an over-arching shared identity.

Identity can be fostered using distinctive objectives, legacy, icons, images, stories, group ethics, routines, behaviours, clothing and social events.

Reinforce the identity and bonds through social activities away from the workplace.

The most powerful identities are often those that come from within the team, both past and present - rather than a created identity that has simply been handed down.

The strength of the bonds between people in a team is a reflection of the depth of their shared experience. The most powerful experiences are felt when there have been:

➢ Clarity of purpose and what success looks like
➢ Clear time lines for preparation, delivery and achievement
➢ Sense of challenge, adversity, achievement and pride
➢ Strong element of energy and enjoyment
➢ Strong sense of belonging, team work and mutual support
➢ Good trust, delegation and focus on positive learning
➢ Review, recognition and celebration of achievements

The deeper the bonds between team members, the stronger the levels of collective commitment, passion and performance. The strength and resilience of team bonds is often what distinguishes the level of performance between teams.

Team members must have a sense of inclusion and belonging.

The team must recognise and appreciate the individuals within it.

Although team members need to operate within a clear framework, the leaders must endeavour to set the conditions so that each person is able to flourish and offer the maximum contribution dependent on their role and abilities.

Most teams contain 3 broad sorts of people:

Self-Starters Need little encouragement
Positive forward thinking outlook
Highly likely to engage and seek improvement

Triers Influenced by the dominant group dynamic
Pick up on the motivations of others
May engage, but probably not openly

Minimalists Just want to get by, likely to do the minimum
Unlikely to seek improvement
May try to hold the team back

Teams should be diverse intellectually, morally and in terms of personalities in order to facilitate openness, initiative, creativity, positive debate, resilience and engagement.

The leader's role is to ensure that the Self-Starters are the dominant influence within the group. An endeavour may fail when the influence of the Minimalists becomes pre-eminent, dominating the group energy and decision making.

In finding an effective mix, teams must avoid intellectual and moral uniformity.

Find and celebrate the un-sung heroes.

The most successful teams explore different views, options and perspectives as a matter of routine. Challenge and debate are essential, as long as the process remains positive and forward thinking.

Team culture and practice must enable alternative views to be heard, considered and acted upon when appropriate.

Keep conversations positive, explorative and focussed on finding solutions rather than identifying problems.

Most teams have many of the answers within them. The leader must find ways to draw out that knowledge, experience, information and ideas.

Even when the team believes it has the right answer, there must be ways to test and rehearse the proposal, in order to ensure that it is not suffering from group-think or lack of challenge and analysis.

Leaders should create an atmosphere where team members feel able to participate actively and are ready to take responsibility.

Once decisions are taken, the group must respect and support those decisions, until the next appropriate time for debate and discussion.

In facing a challenge, the team needs to be prepared and brought up to the right 'operating temperature'. There should be a deliberate approach that gradually matches the intensity to the challenge. Once through the challenge, the group should be allowed to ease back and recuperate.

People and teams need time to think, recuperate and breathe.

The key is to judge when to rev the team up and when to take the foot off the pedal.

As far as you are able, always aim to end on a high. Before putting the team under pressure, have ways to lift them towards a positive end.

Effective teams foster positive relationships with wider teams that have related goals.

Foster and develop your potential successors. The mark of any leader is the impact they have when they are gone.

Energy

Energy is contagious. Passion and enthusiasm are catching.

People are strongly influenced by the energy and vitality of the group around them.

People are always capable of doing more than they imagine.

A group must generate energy to move. That energy can be positive or negative ... forwards or backwards.

Some people are net energy generators while others are net energy drainers. A group is likely to have the following energy map:

Generators   Contributing net energy
Bring positive energy to the group

Neutrals   Neutral energy contributors
Influenced by the group around them

Drainers   Drawing net energy from the group
May bring negative energy

Successful teams are built around a mix of people with net positive collective energy, where they feed off each other's motivation and commitment - creating a positive virtuous cycle.

A group may generate net positive collective energy by drawing on the energy generating individuals within it.

A group may experience net negative collective energy through the draining influence of individuals within it.

The dynamic of a group and situation can be changed by one person stepping forward and taking positive action.

Teams need individuals with skills, experience, competence, resilience and endeavour. However, these alone are not enough. Those characteristics may see a team through a short term challenge but are not sufficient for long term success. Energy and spirit are pre-eminent.

People respond to positive incentives. The more powerful the incentive, the more powerful the effect. Find out what people really care about and what incentives they will respond to.

Celebrate and reward success.

Change

Life is change. Nothing stays the same.

Doing is change.

Leadership is the decisive element in making sustained change.

Foster a mind-set that sees change as part of the everyday and recognises the opportunities within such an approach.

Lead change through the day-to-day.

A key function of leadership is managing the pace of change.

The timing of change is often more important than the change itself.

Leaders must set out the intended direction, engage and inspire people, help explain and understand the change, monitor progress, keep things on track and celebrate the achievements along the way.

You have to work with what you have in front of you, point people in the right direction and help them understand the implications of the different options.

Engage, explain … repeat.

Through change, leaders must be consistent and coherent.

Be clear and honest about the purpose of change:

➤ Reducing costs and resources
➤ Improving performance
➤ Staying ahead of the competition
➤ Responding to a challenge or crisis
➤ Re-organising - adding, changing or removing parts

Change the process and the culture will follow.

Incremental change avoids the risk of complete failure.

Organise change in bite-size chunks. Such changes are easier to understand and there is more chance of success. Each successful step will build the momentum.

Major change increases the risk that is it not well defined, complicated to deliver, fails in part and momentum stalls.

Internal boundaries often get in the way - find ways to encourage people to see flexibility as part of the solution and their future.

Directed autocratic change may have short term benefits, but at long term cost.

Change without thought, planning, control and leadership is random movement.

To embed change, make a simple change and maintain the focus until it is done. Then make another change.

Avoid making too many changes at once.

CHAPTER 7

Success

Success is built on momentum

Momentum is a rhythm

Winning is forged from a desire deep inside

The winning formula is will, belief, skill and self-control

A Reflection on Success

Between 2004 and 2007, Northern Ireland provided a setting so uncertain, fluid and hostile that it was hard for me to know what success and winning looked like.

I had the privilege of commanding the engineer regiment in Northern Ireland. The political Peace Process was in full swing, but not always progressing in straight lines. At times, it was hard to tell the difference between friendlies and enemies. On the ground, periods of relative calm would be shaken by sudden bouts of intense community disorder and rioting. Some dissident groups wanted no part in the political process and terrorist attacks continued almost weekly, with the aim of killing members of the security forces. The annual summer 'Marching Season' was a source of intense inter-community conflict. A series of hotly contested parades saw one side trying to march along a traditional route while the other side did their best to block the parade. The paramilitary and dissident groups would exploit the community tensions. It was difficult to predict which parades would pass peacefully and which ones would explode into violent rioting with the widespread use of flares, fireworks, catapults, bricks, petrol bombs, pipe bombs and firearms.

Through this turbulent time, I led the only engineer regiment in the Province. The regiment provided teams of engineers to support the Police Service of Northern Ireland and the Army with controlling public order. The public order teams could move burning barricades with armoured bulldozers and block roads with heavy obstacles (concrete filled shipping containers). The most dangerous role in the regiment was held by the specialist 'high risk' search teams. The search teams would deploy into areas where terrorist improvised explosive devices (known as IEDs) were believed to have been laid. Their role was to find the devices or prove that the area was clear. They would find themselves searching at all times of the day and night, in all weathers, along roads, railways, gardens, roundabouts, hedges, culverts and even sewers. The teams were regularly shot at by dissidents and stoned by local youths, whilst trying to find sophisticated IEDs designed to kill or maim the people trying to clear them. On the lighter side, the regiment was capable of undertaking any 'civil engineering' task that the security forces needed, such as constructing, renovating or dismantling security force bases in towns, villages, rural hilltops and along the border.

By 2004, the Army was anticipating an end to the Troubles in Northern Ireland and had earmarked the regiment for a move to the mainland near Cambridge for a new Air Support role (building airfields for the Royal Air Force). I arrived in Antrim in October 2004, wondering how to lead the regiment, what objectives to set, how to train, what priorities to follow and how to explain everything to the soldiers and their families. It was hard to pin down what success would look like for the regiment in 2005.

I spotted an opportunity to enhance the regiment's identity and build confidence when I attended a dinner night hosted by the infantry battalion stationed in Hollywood, just outside Belfast. The infantry battalion had a proud boxing tradition. Over a glass of Bushmills whiskey near the end of the evening, the infantry Commanding Officer was keen to secure a warm-up for his boxing team, before they entered the Army's prestigious inter-unit boxing competition. I could tell that he considered our engineers to be a relatively easy opponent. He judged that his boxers would gain valuable experience in the ring, without too great a risk of defeat. A date was set for June 2005.

Fortunately, he did not know that Sergeant 'Geordie' Cook had recently arrived in the regiment and was a champion boxing coach. I sat down with Sergeant Cook the next day and asked him what he needed to win the contest. I then presented Sergeant Cook's plan to my command group. We all needed to commit to the boxers training programme. There could be no half measures. We either set out to win it or we politely declined the invitation from the infantry. The command group agreed unanimously. Sergeant Cook held trials, selected a squad and the boxing team was allowed 5 months of full-time training. As a further incentive, I invited the Engineer-in-Chief (the most senior engineer in the Army) to attend the boxing evening and offer his support to the boxing team.

The evening arrived. The infantry battalion had laid on a good show in their gymnasium with a military band, goat mascot, pipers and a light show. The whole battalion turned out to cheer on their boxers. They clearly anticipated a victory on their home turf. However, the battalion got a sense of what was coming when the whole of the engineer regiment arrived in a fleet of buses and poured out on to the battalion's parade square.

Our engineer corporals and sergeants were fired up and positioned themselves in amongst our soldiers around the boxing ring. The battalion did not know what hit them. Our engineers out-shouted, out-sang and out-supported the infantry soldiers. The atmosphere was electric. Our boxers demolished the infantry boxers, winning 8 of the 9 bouts. It was almost a white-wash. What an amazing evening. The engineer supporters were in a state of euphoria and I had to work hard to remain passive and respectful to our hosts. The Engineer-in-Chief was delighted.

When we arrived safely back at our barracks in Antrim, I finally let go my emotions and shared a few choice words with the regiment to describe the performance of the boxers and our supporters. Even then, I did not fully appreciate that a night of boxing would bring an intensity to the bonds of comradeship within the regiment that would see us through the turbulence and dangers of the coming summer.

By July 2005, we had completed the public order training needed to be ready to support the police through the Marching Season. However, this year was meant to be different. The Army was expected to play a very limited role and the police were expected to shoulder most of the responsibility. In order to keep our engineers motivated, I had begun a programme of conventional engineer training aimed at the future Air Support role on the mainland.

However, events do not always run as expected. The first major contentious parade in Belfast did not go well. The Army was held back in their barracks. The police struggled to maintain order and the nationalist stewards struggled to control their youth. Bricks, golf balls and spark plugs rained down on the loyalist Orange Order parade, who had been squeezed into a narrow marching channel. The loyalist politicians were incensed. The tension and anger within the loyalist communities exploded when the Independent Parades Commission decided that the Orange Order could not march along their historic route past the Ardoyne area of Belfast, known as the Whiterock parade. They were incensed that republican violence had been rewarded with a restriction on an important loyalist parade. Dire warnings of widespread disorder came through to the police and Army.

The Army were called out on to Belfast's streets with instructions to uphold the Parades Commission ruling and block the march at all costs. Our public order teams were in the front line, placing obstacles across the roads to block the march. There was no room for error. The parade had to be stopped, otherwise there would have been serious political consequences. In the event, the Orange Order called off the Whiterock parade. It seemed that the Parades Commission had won through. At the time, no-one forecast that we would be back in Belfast within 2 months facing a conflagration of violent disorder and rioting that would become known as the Whiterock Riots.

By early August 2005, the Marching Season seemed all but over, the regiment breathed a sigh of relief and I headed off on summer leave. A few days later I was driving my family through a white-washed Spanish village when I heard the news on the radio announcing 'Normalisation' in Northern Ireland. I pulled over to the nearest public telephone box and telephoned the regiment's operations room in Antrim. It was true, the political process had moved forward and the government had suddenly agreed to 'normalise' the military presence in Northern Ireland down to peace time garrison levels. In other words, a 2-year clock had started ticking for the Army to dismantle all of the military infrastructure directly related to the Troubles. The political intention was that the Army would no longer support the police routinely by August 2007.

I left my family to complete the holiday in Spain, took a flight back to Belfast and reported to the Army headquarters in Lisburn on Monday morning, ready to receive formal orders from the General Officer Commanding. I was usually positioned in the second or third row of those orders groups, with the front row occupied by the brigade commanders. This time, the General called me to the front and sat me in the middle of the front row. I felt quite awkward. He declared that the engineers would be responsible for the critical path of 'Normalisation'.

We had to dismantle all of the watch towers, patrol bases and border check points across the Province against a timeline that could not be changed. The first stage would be in Belfast and South Armagh. We had to get everyone back to Antrim from their summer holidays, set up forward logistics areas in Belfast and South Armagh, figure out how to dismantle the armoured towers and bases that had been in situ for many years, give engineer orders and deploy out on to the ground. We managed to get the first engineer teams on site within 5 days, a remarkable achievement.

Belfast was still very dangerous with dissident groups taking shots at us and so we had to drive to the working sites in armoured patrol vehicles during the hours of darkness. It was too dangerous to drive through South Armagh due to the threat from roadside bombs. We had to fly in and out by helicopter. The dismantled material had to be flown out underneath a Chinook helicopter.

Northern Ireland was always full of surprises. We had been in South Armagh for 10 days dismantling an armoured patrol base on a hill top overlooking Crossmaglen, when I received a message to return immediately to Army headquarters in Lisburn. The delayed Whiterock march was to be re-run and the Parades Commission had decided to allow it to pass a contentious corner of the nationalist Ardoyne area. Serious disorder was expected. I returned to South Armagh to explain to the regiment that they had to leave their tools and return to Antrim to be equipped for riot control. Events were moving quickly. We flew everyone back to Antrim, issued riot gear, warmed up the vehicles, gave orders and conducted rehearsals. We were ready to go in 2 days.

The Whiterock parade descended into Province-wide rioting for 3 continuous days. The riots were organised and orchestrated by paramilitary groups. On the first day (Saturday 10th September 2005), 1000 police officers and 1000 soldiers were deployed into Belfast. The rioting spread to other towns across Northern Ireland. Over 3 days of rioting, 115 shots were fired at the security forces, 146 blast bombs were thrown and 116 vehicles were hijacked. The number of petrol bombs and bricks thrown at police and Army lines were too numerous to count. A total of 80 police officers were injured. The engineer teams found themselves on the front line, placing obstacles to keep the loyalist and nationalist rioters apart.

By the third night, the loyalist Shankhill Road in Belfast had become a no-go area for the police. The road had been blocked with a series of barricades made of burning cars, vans and buses. By 3.00 a.m. in the morning, the rioters were exhausted and the streets were relatively quiet. The police and Army arrived in force at the entrance to the Shankhill Road. The convoy was led by 2 engineer teams with armoured bulldozers. The bulldozer operators were safe in their armoured cabs. The police and infantry soldiers remained in their armoured patrol vehicles, ready to respond to any trouble. Meanwhile, the whole convoy was led by Corporal 'Taff' Evans walking on foot with a radio in his hand. He had to direct the bulldozer operators by radio, keeping his eyes on the area around the bulldozer so that no civilian would get hurt. I marvelled at the courage and calmness of Corporal Evans, who had been in South Armagh only 5 days earlier dismantling a military patrol base as part of the Peace Process.

Calm returned to Northern Ireland, as the rioters ran out of energy and ammunition. The regiment returned to barracks in Antrim. After a day of rest, the engineers returned to South Armagh to continue dismantling the watchtowers and patrol bases. The political timeline for the first stage of Normalisation only gave the regiment until 31st January 2006 to remove 3 major patrol bases from the hills around Crossmaglen (the heart of what had become known as Bandit Country). The engineer teams worked like Trojans and the work was completed before Christmas. Through all of the turbulence, urgency and pressure, there had not been a single site safety incident. That safety record was a testament to the calm professionalism of the engineers.

In the first week of 2006, news came through that the regiment had to prepare a troop of engineers to reinforce the commando engineer squadron that would be deploying to Afghanistan in the summer. We had become used to surprises.

Through this turbulent, chaotic and dangerous period, the enemy appeared on all sides and the priorities changed dramatically, and suddenly. How did we sustain ourselves when the objectives were not always clear, the definition of success was opaque and the notion of winning had very different interpretations? The answer had been to focus on the basics and do them really well. We spent a lot of time and effort building the engineer teams through challenging training, sports competitions and social events. The training programme was progressive, encouraged calculated risk taking, accepted mistakes, focussed on lessons and built intensity up to realistic levels. The riot training exercises were often more intense and arduous than a night on the streets of Belfast.

A collective feeling of confidence and success was built through a rhythm of training where minor successes were recognised, effort rewarded, positive mind-set celebrated and high standards expected. We built a distinct and powerful regimental identity that bonded everyone around the notion of being world-leaders. We all believed that no-one else in the world could do what we were doing on the streets of Belfast and in the hills of South Armagh. A winning foundation was established through strong team bonds, a powerful identity, an energetic mind-set and a growing rhythm of success.

We felt ready for anything, anywhere, at any time.

Success

The will to succeed is the starting point for success. Then comes persistence.

Belief is everything.

Belief comes from within ... borne of identity, cohesion, determination, confidence, self-control and success.

Success is a mind-set.

It is commitment not motivation that matters.

If you dare not, you will not.

Leaders must define what success looks like.

Few things are more powerful than success. It breeds confidence, strengthens identity and generates momentum.

Devise ways to build confidence and generate success.

Simple steps will be within your control. People must be able to see them in their mind's eye. Larger steps will be more of a challenge and may only be possible from a platform of earlier successful steps.

Success comes in many forms. Identify what is most important to the group, such as:

- ➢ Upholding a set of values or standards
- ➢ Delivering a high quality service
- ➢ More points on the scoreboard than the opponent
- ➢ A rewarding experience
- ➢ Feeling proud of a performance
- ➢ Higher levels of profit than a comparative period

Build the performance and success will follow.

Momentum is a feeling, a rhythm, an energy. Understand and nurture it. People must feel it.

Build success in steps. Plan and prepare. Identify challenging goals that are achievable. Monitor and record progress. Reward and celebrate success.

At each stage, people should have a clear aiming point.

Keep people focussed on the process in front of them and the outcome will take care of itself. Avoid too much focus on the end result.

Focus on the positive actions that need to be completed, rather than the negative actions to be avoided.

Reinforce success. When you win, sit down and figure out what went right. Capture it. Build on it.

Learn more from success than from failure.

Confidence builds through positive reinforcement. Too much critique, however well intentioned, saps confidence.

A group with inherent confidence built on success, can overcome failure and setbacks. Without such depth, setbacks can lead to a negative downward cycle.

Examine errors, mistakes and faults. Address them but do not dwell on them. Move on.

Treat setbacks as challenges.

Sometimes, just surviving and staying together is a good result.

Keep moving. Standing still is not comfortable for long periods.

Always try to take a positive memory forward.

Winning

The greatest teams do the simple things really well, under the greatest pressure.

Challenging to win … inspires and energises.

Winning needs all of the leaders pulling in the same direction.

It is possible to win well.

It is possible to lose well … content with the preparation, commitment and performance.

Do the simple things really well.

There is little value in expecting (and accepting) to lose.

Winning badly will be remembered as just that.

Bear in mind that the right answer is sometimes 'No'.

Challengers and Opponents

Once an adversary knows they are your opponent, the challenge will be twice as hard as it might have been.

It is as important to understand your opponent as it is to know your own people.

It is always preferable to achieve your goal without damaging conflict and the risks that come with it.

Remember that strategy, diplomacy and politics are more powerful when backed up by the capability and will to act.

Deceive and confuse your opponent. Obscure your true intent and plan, locations, tactics and actions.

Conceal your true level of skill, ability and capability.

Study the opposition and learn to think like them. Put their mind-set and potential (re)actions at the heart of your planning and preparations.

Before taking a decision or action, consider your opponent's potential response.

You need information, information, information.

Study your opponent's:

- ➤ Goals, objectives, priorities
- ➤ Mind-set, identity, determination
- ➤ History, legacy
- ➤ Leadership
- ➤ Locations
- ➤ Capabilities, training, techniques
- ➤ Resources
- ➤ Timelines
- ➤ Weaknesses, mistakes, failures

Expect the unexpected.

When something looks and feels wrong, it probably is.

Look for the absence of the normal.

Look for the presence of the abnormal.

Always endeavour to secure and hold the initiative.

If you have the time, test your intended decision or action against your opponent's potential responses.

Knowing when to avoid conflict is as important as knowing when to initiate conflict.

If you must act, be decisive and strike where un-expected. Timing is key.

If your opponent strikes first, try to avoid the blow, saving your energy and strength for your own actions.

If successful, do not go further than you need. Be honourable, compassionate and respectful. Your success will be reinforced and will not become a cause for passionate revenge.

If unsuccessful, cut your losses, withdraw, review and find a way around. Save your energies for another day.

Ensure you have options in the event of failure.

Avoid pyrrhic victories, where there is little of value left at the end.

Mistakes and Failure

The underlying risk in success is complacency.

Admitting your own mistakes and sharing your own vulnerabilities can strengthen the bonds with your team. Take care with the timing and manner of such sharing.

Aim to maintain high performance and managed pressure.

High performance and high pressure can lead to burn out, which may happen suddenly without warning.

Low performance and low pressure can lead to dis-engaged and de-motivated people.

Build resilience through exhaustive contingency planning. You may feel that you have everything in place and people are prepared. However, random, rare and bizarre events do occur. How will you handle the genuinely un-expected?

Mistakes and failure can be powerful moments on the route to success. Success from setbacks.

Failure through managed experimentation can be a powerful engine for improvement.

Avoid over-optimism ... of people and plans. Be honest. Have the courage to change a failing course.

Avoid over-pessimism ... of people and plans. Most people will out-perform your expectations if you engage them, invest in them and give them room to flourish.

Be honest when you do well ... and when you do not.

After identifying the lesson, the biggest challenge is usually to make the change needed to avoid repetition.

Discourage people from looking for excuses. Honest and open review will allow the lessons to be found.

Deal with what went wrong and then focus on the positives, building a sense of improvement, progress and momentum.

Build on the positives, but avoid empty and superficial praise.

Avoid the language of blame.

Fear of failure can dramatically reduce the potential level of performance. People may choose to play it safe rather than risk failure.

Too much focus on mistakes can build a sense of inevitable failure. Negatives can become reinforcing.

The same mistake twice is unfortunate and needs to be highlighted.

The same mistake a third time must be held to account.

Any mistake or failure from lack of effort or care should not be acceptable.

Negativity and pessimism develop in clusters. If an unhappy cluster develops, take action before it spreads.

CHAPTER 8

Military Leadership

*Soldiers may be motivated by the nation and the cause,
but they fight for the comrades beside them*

Military units are a reflection of their leaders ….. good or not

Command is distinct from leadership

Command and leadership should be entwined

A Reflection on Military Leadership

There are few civil leaders who could not learn from the hard won lessons of military leadership ... provided they are open to such learning.

The military is a profession of arms. Leaders should embrace their profession.

Military leadership is tested in the most demanding environments, where the consequences can be fatal.

Military deployments may last for long periods, with leaders and units experiencing extensive pre-deployment training prior to an operational deployment.

Relatively few civil leaders experience such an intense leadership environment, with such direct consequences, for such extended periods. Fortunately, they have the opportunity to learn the lessons without sharing the risks.

Command

Command is the authority that comes with a formal military command appointment.

Command is not leadership ... ideally, they are entwined.

Command is a privilege which comes with rights and powers. The responsibilities must always be paramount.

Use the chain of command. Your subordinate commanders are there to command and lead, not just be instructed.

The more empowered and resilient your subordinate commanders, the more effective that your unit will be.

When you take over command, ask what your predecessor did not have time to complete.

In addition to formal orders and planning meetings, hold informal groupings of key advisers where conversations are open, issues explored, opinions offered, judgements debated and limits of knowledge shared. The more you are able to draw on key advisers, the more you will understand the true position and make effective decisions.

Articulate your vision, intentions and objectives. Review them whenever the situation changes.

The commander must make the final decision and issue clear instructions.

A key skill is the ability to anticipate the needs of the superior commander. Think ahead, consider the potential scenarios and options. Do not wait to be instructed to plan ahead. Anticipate how to be in the right place at the right time, with the right capabilities. If you wait to be told, it may already be too late.

Find information sources who are going to tell you the facts unrestrained and unfiltered, rather than tell you what they think you want to hear.

Get the people management and reporting right. It shows commitment and generates respect.

Leading

Service is at the heart of military leadership.

You get out what you put in. Positive, energetic and forward looking leaders produce positive and spirited people.

Be relaxed but never casual.

Trust is at the core of leadership. Without trust, you are reliant on the authority of command.

Be genuine in your commitment and professionalism. Insincerity will be apparent to everyone, except perhaps you.

Know your people - when they are happy, when they are down, what makes them bored and what fires them up.

Be accessible - to get your message over and receive feedback.

Do not talk across people, just because you can.

Learn to trust your instincts. If you feel uncertain, then stop and think.

Foster and celebrate the distinctive attributes that set the unit apart - operational mission, level of readiness, heritage, values and standards, comradeship, dangers faced.

Generate comradeship, identity and spirit at all levels. Provide an environment for units and sub-units to foster positive inter and intra unit competitiveness, within an over-arching identity.

Daily routines and administration bring many demands and distractions. Keep people focussed on the operational mission.

If you must put the unit under pressure, make sure you have a way to lift them out of it. Always end on a positive.

When making visits, use a relatively 'light touch' in order to avoid generating defensive reactions. Most issues identified during visits can be addressed in slower time through the chain of command.

Safety issues or ill-discipline should be addressed in the immediate moment.

When making formal inspections, ensure that everyone has had the opportunity to know what is expected and has had the time to complete the preparations. Expect the appropriate standards to have been achieved. Address any failures to achieve the standards.

Press to Test - use questions to test the accuracy and objectivity of information being offered. Hesitant or un-clear answers should lead to further examination.

Ensure you have an open door, but take care that it does not undermine the chain of command. People should ensure that their chain of command is aware of any issue before they raise it with you, unless the issue is of a personal nature or involves the people in the chain of command.

When to lead from the front - always, sometimes, never? There is no simple answer, it requires judgement. People must not feel they have been forgotten. Forward presence at the right time and place can have a decisive effect. However, being too far forward too often can lead to narrow vision.

Do not go looking for a fight. Understand the potential consequences. When a fight comes to you, strike hard, do not pull your punches, put the enemy down and step back from the fight as soon as the task is achieved. Do not draw out conflict any longer than necessary.

Respect people's personal space, but ensure there are no no-go areas.

Headquarters

A headquarters must speak and act with a coherent voice. Internal communication is key. The headquarters staff must be encouraged and trained to ensure their actions are in keeping with the commander's intent and instructions, or to seek further clarification.

Subordinate units should not have to contend with disjointed and inconsistent actions from their superior headquarters.

Actions and communication should follow the correct chain of command, taking care not to bypass those lines.

A headquarters should be alive to instances when subordinate units receive instructions from external sources. In such instances, the headquarters should add value with further comment and direction, rather than simply acting as a post box and passing information along.

Maintain continuous awareness of what is going on so that you are able to react quickly to a changing situation.

Intervene only when you have to ... and do so decisively.

Understand that resistance is often found in the middle.

Resources and logistics come first ... and last.

A headquarters must generate a sustainable programme while minimising their interference in subordinate unit programmes.

A headquarters must be conscious of the need for a rhythm that delivers periods of recuperation between the higher tempo operations and commitments.

A headquarters must avoid adding short notice activities into subordinate programmes unless there are sound reasons for doing so. When a short notice activity must be imposed, a supporting explanation should be offered.

The key to the effectiveness of staff advice and debate is accuracy. The headquarters staff must clearly indicate when their input is based on objective knowledge or information. When there is a significant element of subjective judgement, the limitations of that judgement must be made clear.

Get out of the office, see for yourself.

Liaison should be top down - the commander should be visiting the troops, not the other way around.

How you configure at the start of a campaign will directly limit the structure and organisation of operations later on.

The Boss

Be honest. Make clear the limits of your knowledge and understanding, so that account can be taken of the potential gaps. Trust, once lost, takes time to recover.

If in doubt, ask for further direction and guidance. It is better to seek advice, than keep quiet and get it wrong. Do not bluff it out - you may achieve a short term gain, but at the risk of a long term loss of trust.

Do not be a sycophant. It may feel good, but is unlikely to gain you respect.

If you are going to challenge or push back, do your research and pick the right moment.

Be pro-active in offering times and places for your boss to visit. Ensure that your subordinates are doing the same for you.

When the boss comes into a room, do not rush over. Take your time, they will come to you.

Orders

Commanders must exercise their own competence in preparing, giving and adjusting orders.

Do not assume that you always know more than your subordinates. Seek their advice and input before giving orders.

When you receive orders, you should be clear about the higher intent, aim, specified tasks, implied tasks, freedoms, constraints and resources. If any of these are unclear, then make every effort to clarify them. Ask.

Always consider the Most Likely and the Worst Case options.

At all levels, commanders should back-brief their intended plan to their superior commander before initiating action. The purpose must be to ensure that there have been no errors in translation or mis-understandings.

Central co-ordination is key to successful action.

Once orders have been given and actions are underway, monitor events closely in order to be able to respond quickly and effectively to significant changes in the situation.

Intervene only when you have to, but do so decisively.

Keep your superior commander informed. If in doubt, inform and report. If too much information is being passed up, this will soon become apparent. Better that, than have to be chased for information.

Comradeship

Comradeship is at the heart of fighting strength.

Military men and women should feel that their commander values them above all others.

A close knit, cohesive and spirited group can achieve most challenges and bear most hardships.

The generation of ethos, shared identity and fighting spirit requires the continuous attention of the commander.

Discipline

Discipline creates a safe and stable environment for people to live, work and develop. It also generates the confidence that things will be done when and how they need to be done.

All ranks must practice 'appropriate formality'. People should know when to be formal and when they may be more relaxed. This requires judgement, maturity and practice. Commanders must take responsibility for developing this judgement in themselves and their subordinates.

Make sure you look the part - bearing, clothing, equipment.

Your people should look the part. Develop a culture where your unit strives to look professional.

Act the part - as an individual and as a group.

Play the part - support and respect each other.

Military discipline relies on self-discipline at all levels. People must be responsible for their own actions.

Commanders at all levels are responsible for the actions of their group, as well as any others in their presence.

Every level in the chain of command must take responsibility for the maintenance of effective discipline within themselves, their subordinates and their peers, at all times.

If all levels are effectively policing themselves, people should not get themselves into too much trouble.

Be on time and allow for potential hold ups. If you are going to be late, inform people as early as possible.

POSTFACE

You

You only live this life once, embrace it as you pass through it.

Life is 99.9% memories and 0.1% the current moment. Foster and nurture your memories.

Your memories are a treasure.

Live your life. That's not to say you should live it at high speed or take undue risks. Quite the opposite, notice and enjoy the small things.

While focusing on what 'to do', remember 'to be'.

Enjoy yourself.

Take the time, often no more than passing moments, to appreciate what's around you. See the beauty, the potential and the opportunities.

The journey of life is easier with a partner, family and friends. Keep them at your centre. Look after them.

Everyone has a part to play in the life around them. Shape it. Make a difference to your family, friends, colleagues and the people around you. You don't need to change the world, but do aim to leave a mark, something to be proud of.

Give more than you take out - energy, support, positivity, help, learning, compassion, improvement.

Look after yourself. Leadership is best exercised from a position of health, strength, safety, security and calmness.

Find the time to exercise regularly - it will help keep you sane and give you time to think.

Do not work late for the sake of it. People are not fooled. Unless there is a good reason, leave work on time.

Sleep well. Look after yourself in the long term by getting enough good sleep.

If you are facing a heavy workload, rise to the challenge, but make sure you have plans for how you will bring it back to a more sustainable level.

Join **The Real Leadership Forum** Facebook group

Share in the experiences of members

Listen to ideas

Find out what works ... and what does not

Build momentum, vitality and success

Grow together

https://www.facebook.com/groups/thepursuitofrealleadership/

Printed in Great Britain
by Amazon

64007838R00092